THE GRASS
was always
GREENER

THE GRASS

was always

GREENER

ANGELA CLAYSMITH JENKINS

HiP
HISTORY INTO PRINT

First published by
History into Print, 56 Alcester Road,
Studley, Warwickshire B80 7LG in 2009
www.history-into-print.com

ISBN: 978-1-85858-323-5

A Cataloguing in Publication Record
for this title is available from the British Library

Typeset in New Baskerville
Printed in Great Britain by
Hobbs the Printers Ltd

 # Contents

This book is dedicated to my sons
Dylan Jenkins and Max Jenkins

Chapter 1

🌿 Greenland Mills, Bridge Street, 🌿 Bradford on Avon

I had replaced my eldest sister as the black sheep of the family. Jean's sin, ironically, was that she was a nun. It was unconventional you see; my parents were embarrassed; they did not like to mention it. But a few years had passed and they had got used to it. Well, they didn't really talk about her now so that solved that problem. I had taken over. Not that I had done anything awful, I was just unconventional: awkward they said.

I had wanted to be a dairy herdswoman for a start; girls shouldn't do hard, mucky jobs. If that was not bad enough I didn't want to go to the ladies agricultural college just four miles away from home, in Redditch, I wanted to go as far away as possible. Devon was the furthest I could make it so I went to Seale-Hayne College near Newton Abbot and took a two year course in Dairying preceded by a two year practical stint on a couple of farms.

My parents did not want me to spread my wings, to explore life, to experience things, to be independent. They wanted me to stay in the nest, in the narrow-minded bosom of the family, sheltered and protected. For as long as I had developed an awareness of the larger world it had always been my ambition to be free of these blinkered restraints.

To make matters worse, and something my mother has never forgiven, I moved miles away from home to start my first job once I had qualified. Their dearest wish seemed to be that I would secure a position as a laboratory technician at Cadbury's chocolate factory about twelve miles from home. I could then commute daily while continuing to live at home. This was the furthest thing from my thoughts. I had experienced folk clubs and jazz, art and design, had my head turned by literature. I had a new boyfriend and I didn't want to lose him, he was special. So: another black mark. I had moved to Wiltshire; by no means the centre of the universe but there I would not lead the claustrophobic, controlled life that I expected at home.

Worse was to come. We had wanted to marry and my boyfriend, Bryn, had to go to Dad, asking permission to get engaged, and to be honest they did not like him. They did not like his artistic side. He painted and wrote poetry, was informed about films and music, especially his great love The Blues. They did not like his personality: gentle and rather shy, retiring in boisterous company. Worst of all Bryn was a socialist; they really hated this. They had refused to acknowledge that I might be interested in politics and when they finally did realise it they assumed that I would follow them into the conservative party and become a true blue. Instead of that I married someone who was damn near a communist.

No; I did not conform; they were disappointed in me. They told me that they had such great hopes of me and I was going astray. Like a sheep I thought. A *black* sheep, surely?

We had returned from our short honeymoon in Paris in September 1965 and set up home in Bradford on Avon, Wiltshire. Our flat was isolated; down the road beside the river and over the railway level-crossing. As a group of mill buildings came into view the sound of the weir became audible. Bryn worked at the printing factory housed in the old buildings and our flat was on the top floor of one of these buildings, tied to the job.

We were delighted to be so isolated. As newly-weds we wanted no other company than our own. That autumn I would arrive home from work by train at Bradford on Avon and walk through the town towards the ancient stone bridge, looking forward to the tree-lined lane to Greenland Mills. I was relieved to leave my job behind and as I walked down the cool lane to the flat, scuffing my feet through fallen lime leaves, I left my cares back in Westbury.

My job as bacteriologist in charge of the laboratory at the processed-cheese factory had become increasingly stressful. I felt that I was being overloaded with work that was not on my job-description. After putting up with it for over a year things finally came to a head when the assistant manager left and I realised that I had been groomed to take on his responsibilities until a new assistant manager had been appointed.

I would have to decide what to do about it but for now I was glad to get back to the flat. We had spent all our available money on the furniture and our wedding presents had been brought down by my parents while we were in Paris and were now installed.

A convector heater and a two-bar fire with a huge curved reflector together with a paraffin stove were our sources of heat. My parents had given us a twin-tub washing machine as our wedding present and Bryn's parents had supplied our gas stove. A low teak coffee table and standard lamp gave the lounge a contemporary look against the walls papered in vibrant flame red and citrus yellow. A loaded bookcase each from our previous bedrooms completed the look.

My books were a varied lot. I had three or four Observers books, my college text books on diseases of animals, soil bacteria and dairy chemistry, some books of poetry and a selection of art books. I had started to develop an interest in both architecture and landscape and was slowly building up a small collection of reference books.

For my fix of fiction I had been avidly reading the novels of Daphne du Maurier and loved the mixture of history, romance and beautifully observed locations. My interests were developing in other ways also: the classic nineteenth-century novels had been on my shelves for a couple of years and the wordy descriptions of Jane Austen, Charlotte Brontë and Thomas Hardy felt very reassuring, but beside these I was enjoying more contemporary fiction such as Mary McCarthy's *The Group*, and Iris Murdoch's *The Sandcastle, Under the Net, The Bell Jar* and *The Severed Head.*

Anyway, any gaps on the shelves of my bookcase were soon filled by Bryn's books – reference books for his model soldiers, biographies of jazz greats, poetry volumes and art books. Our lounge had a very studious yet lived-in look.

All these extras combined with the furniture we had saved-up for during the year we were engaged: the Scandinavian style three-piece-suite, the old rocking chair and the dark brown carpet. We were delighted with our first home and sat by the light of the table lamp gazing with satisfaction at the scene we had created.

Our dining room did not present such a tranquil picture. We had no furniture at all in here but had decided to decorate it in blue and green to enhance the Midwinter tableware we had selected. Various friends and relatives had bought us items from this range which featured stylized bright blue flowers and green leaves against a white background. The teapot- and coffee-pot-lid were plain blue, as were the saucers and we were looking forward to entertaining our first visitors using these smart ceramics.

The walls of the dining room would be crisp white and I had designed an abstract mural to paint on the wall where the most natural light fell. First I had drawn out the design of billowing shapes in my sketch-book then transferred the paisley-inspired cloud and wave forms onto the wall in pencil. Each evening when I returned from work I would fill in another area using bold poster paints. Once the mural was complete I wanted curtains to hang and I decided to try and block-print them myself. We went to the art shop in Bath and bought a slab of thick brown lino and a couple of cutting tools. The pattern was to feature two different, alternating designs to give a chequer-board effect. One was a blue fleur-de-lys on a white background and the other square was a white quatre-foil on a green backing. The next weekend I purchased two yards of white cotton fabric, two tubes of water-resistant ink and a small wooden roller. As a printer, Bryn was keen to oversee the process and offer advice and we set up our home-made pasting table as a work bench. The curtains took all day to print and some of the squares were rather blotchy but the sense of achievement outweighed the imperfections and I was keen for the ink to dry so I could hem the fabric and sew brass curtain rings to the top. In a few days the dining room had a pair of curtains hanging from a quickly improvised pole made out of a garden cane.

The furniture came gradually over the next year and until then we made do with kitchen stools and the paste-table draped with a cloth. This didn't stop us from entertaining and once the room was decorated we gave in to Mum and Dad's pleas to visit us. They reminded us of their own struggle for furniture in their first home together at Astwood Bank in Worcestershire. They seemed glad that I was developing the skills of make, make-do and mend. The flat was duly admired and the visit went off without any scathing words about what we *didn't* have.

Christmas 1965 meant a decision: where do we go for the festive season? We devised a plan to visit each set of parents on alternate years and because we had made less visits to Torquay we started there. I loved these trips; everything was so easy-going; there were so many friends to see; such beautiful walks to take and most of all, nobody was judgemental – we could do our own thing.

Bryn's friend Mike Tolliday had married Vanessa from Sheffield and they had a flat at Ellacombe but we met up in town for a windy walk along the front followed by a piping hot coffee and talked intensely about art and artists. On several autumn weekends Bryn and I had been out in the countryside around Bath sketching the landscape and we chatted to Mike about our styles and techniques.

We would try to fit in a visit to Kevin Ryland to swap film news and compare the programme of our Bath Film Society with Torquay. In his den we talked against a background of exquisite classical music playing on the turntable and sometimes Kevin would pause to take up his baton and conduct an exciting passage.

Whenever we could we tried to help Bryn's mother with serving and clearing the meals and with shopping. Mr Jenkins' vague behaviour had been diagnosed as 'premature senility' and Mrs J was finding it increasingly difficult to cope. Despite this, Christmas day was full of traditional fun and we were full of festive food.

Later in the visit we would try to cram in an evening with John Spence or Ron Collier to get our fix of Jazz and finally it was time to pack our bags and catch the train back to Bradford on Avon and work.

I dreaded going to work now. All the excitement and pride was gone. I just felt resentful at being put-on. I had no sense of job satisfaction anymore and I decided that as soon as possible in 1966 I would find a new job.

Meanwhile, New Year brought its usual soul-searching and reflections of the past year and good intentions for the year to come. In an introspective moment I thought about myself and my life. I was beginning to think of myself as a more rounded, complete person yet developing the tolerance it takes to share your life with someone. I thought about my father, a free-thinking philosopher, a practical and skilled man whose confidence had been put down by his step-father and his place in the family usurped by his half-brother and sisters, according to my mother.

My thoughts drifted to my mother whose wildly romantic imagination and artistic skills had been curbed by a domineering and moody father. She had escaped from one controlling man to another when she experienced a difficult first marriage.

As I looked back at my life at the start of a new year inevitably I could see links with my own personality. What wasn't nature was nurture. Yes, I had inherited the practicality, the imagination and the artistic gene but I felt that I too had been controlled and I relished the fact that now I could function as an adult. I resolved to enjoy my life with my wonderful husband, build a nice home together and to develop my interests.

New Year's Day 1966 was also a milestone for my school friend Judy Davies. She married John Naylor, a colleague in the Inland Revenue, at Alvechurch church and then we went to the reception at Hopwood village hall.

I had started to take a brand new magazine, 'Nova' and became quite excited each month when it was due out. I devoured its large-format glossy pages for fashion, make-up tips, interiors and fascinating articles.

Bryn always had a striking sense of fashion with his long black leather coat, tapered trousers and bold shirts and ties and he encouraged me to combine my love of colour with my fast-developing desire to be up-to-the-minute. I favoured black tights and black jumpers with a brightly patterned

Angie, Brandon Hill, Bristol May 1966.

skirt and shoes in a co-ordinating colour. Starting with the emerald green shoes I had worn on honeymoon I had built up a collection ranging from black stilettos to soft turquoise leather flatties laced with a black satin bow.

On Saturdays we would take the train the fifteen miles to Bath Spa and spend the day in bookshops and record stalls or buying art materials and new clothes. We had our usual cup of tea and iced bun at Hands Dairy on Abbey Green or sometimes bought chips in Kingsmead Square. The day would usually be rounded off by a visit to the cinema and a dash down to the station to catch the late train home. For more avant-garde films we attended the Film Society in The Octagon sometimes puzzling over films directed by Luis Bunuel, and Jean Vigo, Fellini or Jean-Luc Goddard.

Sometimes we would visit Bristol and noticed some derelict areas that still looked like bomb sites from the war.

From time to time we would feel obliged to travel to Redditch and visit my parents. We would catch the steam train to Birmingham New Street and transfer onto the Redditch line with the train picking up a token at Barnt Green when it began the single-track part of the journey. The fatted calf was usually killed and we would be made a fuss of by Mum and Dad, Granny and Grandad and both of the aunties and we would exchange family news.

My eldest sister, Jean was a nun at Laleham Abbey near Staines and we had been to see her take her final vows at an emotional service. The Anglican sisterhood of St Peter ran a nursing home for elderly ladies in an annexe of the abbey and Jean's nursing skills were put to use. Strangely though, the nuns were often asked to work in areas they had no experience of, presumably as a trial or test of faith. After a while Jean was detailed to work in the bakery making communion wafers.

Jimmy, my eldest brother was now a sub-mariner and based at Portsmouth. He and Anne were the proud parents of two sons, Jonathan and Russell. One day when the naval dockyard was open we went down for a visit to HMS Dolphin.

Rosemary and Maurice's family had grown too. With Susan and Louise quickly joining Andrew they had moved to a larger house in Studley.

Steve and Margaret were engaged and were hoping to be married next year, 1967.

Mum and Dad couldn't resist trying to tempt us up to the Midlands to be close to them and the family. They seemed to forget that it would be much further from Bryn's home town, and always, in the back of my mind was the anxiety that if I lived close by I would be swallowed up by the family, consumed by expectations, my time with Bryn would be eaten away by visiting and that greedy monster of conformity would wallow unseen in everything we did.

In the spring I decided I really must find another job. My position at Unigate Dairies had become unbearable. What was it to be? Ministry of Agriculture? The Milk Marketing Board? Another dairy? I scoured the situations vacant columns in the papers. Then I saw a possible. There was to be a new university at Bath built on a brand new campus at Claverton Down. The first faculty to open would be the School of Biological Sciences and they were looking for technicians. I wondered if that would fit the bill. After all, my job for the last two years had been in a laboratory. I requested an application form, completed it and secured an interview.

I got the job! I was to be senior technician in the microbiology department. The core of the staff, both academic and technical support had been brought in from a Bristol technical college and I would work with them providing laboratory services for undergraduates and also if the need arose, help with post-graduate research. I felt very excited about this move from manufacturing to academia and could hardly wait to start my new job in May 1966.

The journey was rather a challenge. I caught the train to Bath Spa and walked along Pultney Road to start the long climb up Bathwick Hill. The university was still under construction and scaffolding clad the next phase of the development. I was based in the media preparation-room with large laboratories along the corridor in one direction and smaller labs and offices on the other side. The botany and zoology departments were housed in the same two-storey block.

The technicians were responsible for the production and sterilisation of all the growth media for the study of bacteria, the maintenance of bacterial cultures and the disposal of the cultures once they had been grown and examined. We also serviced all the laboratories and equipment and kept a huge stock room and refrigerated area full of anything that would be needed by the teaching staff.

I was in my element: I could organise, draw up rotas, plans and timetables. Everything had its place – that was important – and I could label and colour-code to my hearts content. However, there was a fly in the ointment and it was one I had already experienced in my previous job. I was in a position senior to staff that knew the job inside out, could probably do it blindfold. Once again I would need tact and diplomacy to keep the team on my side.

Once I had a new and demanding job I started to feel better and could start some projects at home that I had just been shelving. We decorated our bedroom in a primrose yellow colour over coarse woodchip paper. The room looked light and fresh and the colour enhanced the bright orange blanket and bedspread we had been given by Auntie Daye for a wedding present. We decided we could afford to buy some proper bedside cabinets now and chuck out the wooden orange boxes we had been using. We had stood the boxes on end and covered the top with a tray cloth to make a base for our lamps. The central division formed a shelf. I smiled when we chose our Liden whitewood cabinets from Haskins store at Shepton Mallet; they were almost identical to the orange boxes in shape, size and style.

While we were at the store we also chose two whitewood chests of drawers to paint white with yellow drawer fronts. We planned to link these together with a piece of fablon-covered plywood to form a dressing-table; an old mirror could ledge on top. Our home was gradually coming together.

The summer loomed and we talked about places we would like to visit and things we would like to do. Our first winter together had been wonderful. Our isolated flat would resound to the music of Charlie Parker, Albert Ammons and Bessie Smith. I had tried to teach Bryn some ballroom dancing steps. We'd put some strict tempo big-band on the turntable and opened up our door onto the long landing giving us a forty foot gangway to practice waltzes and quicksteps with space for a turn at the top of the staircase. Despite his many years of listening to music and his keen appreciation of tempo Bryn never got the hang of formal dance steps and we would end up a giggling heap on the floor.

Some winter evenings we would spend sitting up to our trusty paste-table with reference books propped up under a table lamp. Bryn would instruct me in the craft of uniform making for his model soldiers. He often bought plastic cowboys and Indians and hacked off their holsters and head-dresses with a scalpel and remoulded the figures with plastic wood. From bits of toothpaste tube or tissue paper, wire and wood he carefully crafted new regimental uniforms exactly copied from the colour plates in his books. I might be trusted to form a helmet or cap or maybe a weapon. Hours would pass in intense concentration until our sore eyes could focus no longer and it was time to turn the radio off and go to bed.

Lighter evenings meant we could go out for walks after work and we explored Bradford on Avon, its hills and terraces, its footpaths and canal. Each weekend usually had the same format; Saturdays were spent visiting either Bath or Bristol and Sundays were for walking or sketching. Even although we lived on very little money as we were saving for a house deposit, our lives seemed blissful.

Our first wedding anniversary, September the eighteenth, approached and we decided to take the train to Weymouth for the day. We walked on the sands in a stiff breeze, the lifting sand making my black eye-liner run. As we sat in a café on the sea front I knew I couldn't be happier. Bryn was my mentor. I lived my life through him and his interests. I loved my life and felt fulfilled. It never occurred to me that the personal strength that I had gained in my adolescence and young adulthood was being leached away. I adored and admired him; he was bohemian, cosmopolitan, knowledgeable and spontaneous. To my parents he was still *persona non grata*.

Angie, Weymouth 18th September 1966. First wedding anniversary.

That summer I had introduced him to my Grandma Ancell and all the family in Hastings where we went for a short break. I showed him the landmarks of all my summer holidays with my cousins; I took him to all the places where we had leapt about and explored, as free as the wind while Mum and Dad sat at home and talked about the past with Gran and Auntie. Bryn and I took the cliff railway up the West Hill where I showed him the soft sandstone rocks beneath the ruined castle where my cousins had taught me how to rotate a big penny in the rocks to form a hemi-spherical depression; then we walked over to St Clement's caves and I told him of our visits there as children when Dad had hinted at smugglers. The next day we visited the Old Town and walked past the tall black net-drying huts and sat a while on the beach trying to sketch the East Cliff Railway. My holidays in Hastings all through my childhood were very special; there was a freedom and excitement; I loved being with my cousins splashing in the sea and sun bathing on the pebbly beach and sometimes we would buy paper cones of cockles or mussels to eat with salt and vinegar. Bryn understood all I was trying to convey to him – he had enjoyed a similar childhood but on the sheltered sandy beaches of Torbay.

Later on in the summer Mum and Dad had brought Granny and Grandad Winnett down to Wiltshire for a day. Bryn had now met all the family and I thought his easy going ways had won them all over. But he hadn't quite won over my parents. He wasn't really comfortable with the boisterous banter of our family life. This had become apparent when we spent Christmas in Redditch and Bryn compared it with the quiet time we had spent in Torquay only the week before.

We were glad to return to Bradford on Avon and on New Years Day we set off on a raw grey morning to be tourists for the day and explore the beautiful town. We strode up the lane and carefully crossed the level crossing then walked on up to the top of Bridge Street.

As we walked across the pretty riverside park I glanced back and had a thought.

'Let's take photos of each other with the chapel on the bridge as a backdrop. I remember reading that it dates from the fourteenth century and once was used as a lock-up', I recalled as we posed in the thin sunlight. Before moving off we turned to admire the old mill buildings on the north side of the river which were a remnant of the wool weaving days.

Shoving the camera back into the duffel bag we continued past St Margaret's Hall and across the foot-bridge and up to Holy Trinity Church.

'I wonder if we can find the grave of Herr Shrapnel' Bryn mused as we looked over the wall. 'I think he is buried here.'

Unable to find it we crossed the road to gaze in wonder at the tiny Saxon Chapel of St Laurence.

As we began to weave our way up the steps between the spinners' and cloth-worker's cottages the sun came out and we strolled along Middle Rank basking in the warmth.

'Looks like they are doing a lot of renovation here', Bryn ventured as we noticed that many of the dilapidated and empty cottages had piles of stone blocks and timber piled up outside the shuttered doors.

Finally we reached the top of the hill and Bradford on Avon dripped down the slope like golden honey in a bowl. We crept quietly into the greenly damp and dark church of St Marys Tory built as a hermitage in the fourteen hundreds then relished the contrasting sunlight as we moved outside and leant against the wooden railings to take in the view.

'See if we can spot our flat at Greenland Mills,' I suggested. 'We might have a chance with no leaves on the trees.' Our eyes followed the course of the railway line and we thought we could see the cluster of buildings that formed the printing factory.

It was time to turn for home and at Lower Rank we crossed Newtown, turned down Church Street then took the footpath down through Barton Orchard after admiring some very handsome houses on the way. We crossed the train line after being instructed to Stop, Look and Listen and shortly passed over the ancient looking Barton Bridge. An enormous tithe barn loomed up behind the Barton and we ventured up the track to gawp at its cathedral-like proportions.

'We'll have to do the canal walk another day. I've gone chilly.' I shivered. 'We can have a proper look at the tithe barn too.' I linked my arm through Bryn's as we walked across the playing field. 'Let's walk a bit faster.'

We went briskly along the Frome Road and joined up with St Margaret's Street, down to the bridge and into the rather chill gloom of Bridge Street where it smelt of leaf mould. Once we were back at the flat we made two mugs of tea and four rounds of toast and wondered what 1967 would bring for us.

I had a new and interesting job but Bryn was not so lucky. He had always been a keen union man and wanted to voice his feelings more at the chapel meetings.

'It's so damned Dickensian,' he ranted at me. 'There are so many accidents waiting to happen. Then there are the powder sprays and the toxic inks. I used to take such a pride in the craft of printing but now it seems all that has gone out of the window. I think letter-press printing is on its way out and every thing will turn over to litho.'

'Well do something about it then,' I calmly replied.

'I can't,' Bryn stormed. 'They've got me over a barrel. If I open my mouth to complain I could be out of a job. Don't forget this is a tied flat. No job, no home! What am I supposed to do?'

'Perhaps we should look for somewhere else to live,' I said quietly as I looked wistfully round the flat we had transformed from a cold and dismal property into a delightful bohemian home.

'Where else will there be in Bradford on Avon? Where else could I get a job?' Bryn was feeling negative and I could see the discussion would get nowhere. I tactfully suggested putting some music on and we were gradually lulled into a more tranquil mood by the mellow tones of the Duke Ellington orchestra.

Spring came and went with visits to Torquay and a brief holiday in Wales and then in May, just before my birthday a colleague of mine at the university said she and her husband were giving up their flat in Bath to buy a house in the country. Were we interested? The rent was two pounds a week – ten shillings more than our current flat but we decided to look at it. It was an irresistible location and we decided to rent it. Bryn was delighted; he had started to feel oppressed at work and was beginning to show signs of depression. We organised a removal lorry and waved goodbye to Greenland Mills.

Chapter 2

🌿 Ainslie's Belvedere, Bath 🌿

What a view!' we said in unison as we moved across the enormous room to stand by the huge sash window. We were mesmerised as our eyes roved from the beautiful tree tops in Hedgemead Park at the bottom of the garden, down across Walcot, on to Sydney Gardens and up the slopes of Bathwick Hill crowned by the Sham Castle.

Slowly we readjusted our focus on our immediate environment.

'Look at that sweet little balcony' I cooed as we glanced down at the black ironwork guarding the four-storey drop to the garden below.

'Look at the size of this room,' Bryn enthused as we finally turned our backs on the view. 'It looks even bigger now. We'd better think where we are going to put the furniture.'

'I started to think about that as soon as we decided on it,' I smiled. 'We've only got three rooms. We'll need a table for the kitchen which we can use with our stools and maybe a tall cabinet.' The main door of the flat opened into the kitchen off the first floor landing. The view from the window over the sink wasn't quite as spectacular as it looked down onto the end of Ainslie's Belvedere where the cul-de-sac formed the thin end of a wedge and the next street off Lansdown Hill was built up on an embankment shielded by fir trees.

The bathroom was down two levels in the basement which would mean a long and cold journey to use the facilities. I guessed my candlewick dressing gown would be an essential item, ready on the back of the door. An old geyser heated the water and the lavatory was flushed from an ornate high-level cistern. There was nothing to warm the room so when it was time for our weekly bath we would have to run the taps and make a dash for it making sure we kept submerged under the steaming water for as long as possible. We decided on the first day that we would have our morning wash at the kitchen sink and if necessary use a bucket rather than descend two flights of stairs in the night.

Bryn and I stood with our backs to the ornate fireplace in the magnificently proportioned Georgian room which was to be our bedroom, dining room and lounge all rolled into one. The bed would stand against the back wall with a cupboard each side and our chests of drawers and wardrobe could follow round the walls on each side.

Our tweedy covered three piece suite and coffee table would go in front of the fire place with the standard lamp behind one of the chairs. Our two bookcases could flank the grate and that just left the dining table to think about.

'As we have been using the paste table up until now I think we can ditch that,' I said thankfully. 'What about buying a new dining table and putting it in the kitchen, there's quite a lot of space to fill up. I saw a lovely pine one at Rossiters in Broad Street.'

'We'll have to see how the money goes,' warned Bryn, probably thinking he would not want to compromise his record-buying allowance. 'We could get a second-hand one from Cavill's in the market.'

We lugged into place what furniture we could and made some sandwiches for tea. It would be Monday before the gas man would come to fit the stove.

We had Sunday to add a bit of style to our flat. Luckily the walls were painted a neutral colour and in any case it was written in the lease that we could not decorate them – even supposing we had ladders tall enough to reach the high ceilings. We hung our pictures on the nails; the print of fighting horses by Delacroix, paintings of Bryn's, an abstract oil of Meadfoot Beach given us as a wedding present by Mike Tolliday. Our posters and ornaments would soon find a place.

Almost at once Bryn found a new job. He had scanned the Bath Chronicle and spotted an unusual vacancy. A company that dealt in mail-order stockings and tights wanted a machine manager for their in-house print department. Their premises were very near by, in Walcot Street and Bryn went for an interview.

'The place is in an old school or something,' he explained. 'The buildings are divided between the store rooms and packing department and the printing office. They do everything from the packets and adverts to all the office stationery.'

'Yes, but didn't you say it was litho printing?' I questioned. 'You've only ever done letterpress.'

'That's the good thing. You know how fed up I've got with the old fashioned techniques and this place will actually train me up. Send me on a course. It's up in London and I would be there for five days.' Bryn was full of enthusiasm and wanted to let them know at once that he would accept the job.

It was good to see him looking forward to going to work in the morning. He descended several staircases from our flat passing our bathroom in the basement then down again past the dark and dusty, musty rooms of the sub-basement and out of the substantial back door into the garden. Passing through the garden gate he was in Hedgemead Park and had a delightful walk down to London Road. Once he had crossed over there was just a short walk down Walcot Street and he was there.

Bryn, Snowdonia July 1967.

Things were on the up. We both had jobs that we were happy in, we were earning decent money and we were living in a stylish, thriving city. We had bought a car in the spring, an old upright, mushroom-coloured Ford Popular and although I used it to drive to work at the university on Claverton Down at weekends we preferred to leave it parked outside and walk into town.

Ainslie's Belvedere was half a mile up Lansdown Road and the saunter into town was delightful. We could look out over the city centre as we descended the hill and from the elevated pavement we had a glorious view of the mellow Georgian properties. This close proximity to the city centre made our visits to the Film Society and cinema much easier. Art exhibitions were on our doorstep, the museum and library shared the same site and we could get home from concerts without any inconvenience.

That summer we drove to north Wales and motored round Snowdonia, the first time I had ever seen the impressive mountains.

Having a car also meant an easier journey to both Redditch and Torquay to see our parents. Bryn would catch up on his record buying by visiting Whitnall's at the bottom of the steps in Rock Walk, Torquay, or listen in comfort to a LP track in a booth at Peter Russell's Hot Record Store in Plymouth. In Birmingham the mecca for jazz and blues records was the Diskery with thousands of albums in wooden crates at waist height.

Rather than wait in the shop for hours watching Bryn thumb rack after rack of records I would seek out fabric shops to buy the latest designs in trendy materials to transform into shirts, skirts and dresses. We had been to see the Bridget Riley Op Art exhibition at the Tate Gallery in London and the intricate black and white designs weaving and waving into each other giving a slightly queasy optical effect had been translated onto fabric. A little went a long way and a couple of yards would make a simple shift dress or skirt.

Since the Beatles had issued *Sergeant Pepper's Lonely Hearts Club Band* the fashion industry had been flooded with eastern-inspired paisley patterns and I chose several variations on this theme to make up into shirts for Bryn. I had already tackled these complicated patterns with yokes and wrist plackets, inter-lined cuffs, collar-bands and button-down collars. Bryn was proud of his one-off shirts which looked good under his brown corduroy jacket or leather coat. He was growing his hair a bit longer now but I was not convinced that his wiry, curly hair would suit this style.

I favoured swirling. psychedelic patterns influenced by LSD trips and the hippy summer of love. After a couple of evenings of cutting, pinning and sewing I had a unique dress or skirt.

Twiggy was sporting her demure, uncluttered mini-skirt look and I bought a cream corduroy dress with a lace collar that fastened with two pearl buttons. With cream tights and my flat, brown, Saxone shoes I looked quite fashionable!

Since the resurgence of interest during the early 1960's of William Morris and the re-issue by Sanderson of his fabric designs I had started to buy bric-a-brac with an Arts and Crafts or Art Nouveau style. We would browse round second-hand shops or market stalls wherever we went, whether it was Bath or Bristol, Torquay or Plymouth.

'Hey, look at that funny thing! Whatever is it?' I exclaimed while we were poking about in a cluttered shop in Winner Street, Paignton. Stuck at the back of a shelf was a curvaceous ceramic item in wine-red with a swirling pattern in green, cream, ochre and burnt sienna snaking up each side of a circular opening.

'Surely it's a clock case without the clock,' Bryn suggested, reaching it down.

Inside it was stamped with the place of manufacture: Berlin. A grubby sticker announced the price as five shillings. We handed over our coins and back outside on the pavement agreed that it would make a nice group with the tall copper jug we had bought for fifteen shillings and the pewter vase we had picked up for seven and six. Our Art Nouveau collection was growing and we compared the styles with the illustrations in my Dutton Vista book by Mario Amaya.

Our flat was starting to look like a treasure trove and we had to separate our growing collections according to style. In the big bed-sitting room we arranged our Art Nouveau finds and old bits and pieces that Mum and Dad given us against a back drop of home-made William Morris cushions and table cloths. We had bought a set of posters by Alphonse Mucha called The Four Seasons and displayed them on black plastic poster hangers which only needed a tack or pin in the wall. Encouraged by Mum I had laboriously made a huge lampshade for our standard lamp using a Morris fabric depicting enormous, stylized, emerald green flowers. Each segment of the shade was centred on a flower and as I sewed the fabric to the tape I had bound round the metal frame my fingers were almost bleeding. Once I had stitched in the white silk lining it was time to try it out. The light gleamed through the fabric like a jewel and I soon forgot my sore fingers.

Our pop art and psychedelic posters were taped onto the kitchen doors. Bryn had taken Oz magazine since it had first come out earlier that year and we cut out the outrageous illustrations and displayed them on the walls. One weekend we bought a poster depicting Che Guevara the Marxist revolutionary leader – an image that was to become world famous.

A couple of weeks after Bryn had started at Nylons Unlimited he returned home from work with a suggestion.

'They want to get me on the lithographic printing course in London. Book me into a hotel near the training centre. All expenses paid.' He took a breath and watched for my reaction. 'I wondered if we could wangle you into the hotel and just pay for your share of the expenses. What do you think?'

'Wonderful,' I enthused. 'We've always wanted the chance of a few days in London. It'll be great. Yes, ask them tomorrow.'

A week later we were lugging our suitcases from South Kensington underground station towards the Glencourt Hotel in Onslow Gardens just behind Old Brompton Road.

'What a great location,' Bryn confirmed as we studied our map. 'We're half way between the Kings Road and the museum quarter and Hyde Park's under a mile away. Let's explore for a while this evening.'

The course was due to start in the morning and Bryn would finish at 4pm each day. Over the next five days I visited the Victoria and Albert Museum fascinated by everything Victorian; the Natural History Museum where I took in marvels I never knew existed and wandered intoxicated round the sights of Kensington and Chelsea. In the late afternoon we would meet up and walk along Kensington High Street, Knightsbridge or Kings Road. We browsed round the new Biba store soaking up the ambience of palms, feather boas and exotic lighting, then at the other end of the spectrum we would shuffle sedately across the magnificent Food Hall at Harrods admiring the tiled walls and marble counters loaded with fish, game and spicy sausages and savouring the delicious aroma.

Although we had been there before we could not resist a walk along Carnaby Street on Saturday before we caught the train home from Paddington. Trying not to feel too provincial we edged past the young trendies of London and nudged each other as another outlandishly dressed body swept by in anything from a scarlet guard's tunic to a fringed caftan or a Mary Quant mini.

It seemed dull back in Bath after the rich experiences of the capital and we were eager to talk about it during our visit to Redditch in early July. Nobody was very interested. Steve and Maggie were busy planning their wedding, all my friends were enjoying their mundane and predictable lives and my parents thought that we should be settling down – after all, we had been married almost two years.

'Never mind the sights of London, how did the course go?' Mum queried.

'Are you earning better money now you are properly trained?' Dad wanted to know.

'That skirt's too short,' Mum interjected, irrelevantly.

I did not dare tell them that Bryn was disenchanted with his job already.

'It's so tedious,' he had groaned last week. 'All those flipping pictures of stocking tops and legs. All I do is load the paper, check the ink and the plate, press the button and away it goes. No skill needed. Is that what I did a five year apprenticeship for?'

I let him rant on, not reminding him that two months ago he was fed up with his last job and had complained every evening about the bad working conditions and the fiddly hassle of deckle edges and the embossed script of business cards or the perforations and no-carbon-required paper of invoice books or hundreds of raffle tickets and sale posters. A positive approach was needed.

'Yes, but it's so much cleaner and your wages are higher.' I argued.

'I know the hourly rate is more, but there are no extras for special finishes and virtually no overtime,' he countered gloomily.

As we drove home from Redditch going south via Evesham and Cheltenham I noticed that Bryn was unusually quiet. We had just joined the A46 down towards Stroud when Bryn looked at me and said, 'I wonder if there is anything in what your parents said. They are always telling us that the Midlands are where the money is, that the wages are higher and the cost of living is lower. I know we are sick of hearing that everyone is so affluent, but do you think they have a point?'

I adjusted my hands on the wheel but kept my eyes on the road as it had started to get dark. I could not believe I had heard him correctly. I fought for the right words,

'Doesn't that go against all we believe in? Don't we feel there is more to life than money? Anyway we don't really want to live near my family do we?'

'I know, but they said they would help us and the family would rally round if we were in need. Now we are going to try for a baby it might be sensible to be up there,' Bryn replied. It was obvious that he had been thinking about it.

'We would be much further from your Mum and Dad though,' I put in, trying to keep a balance in the discussion. 'Anyhow we would miss the concerts; we've seen Ravi Shankar, Duke Ellington, Count Basie and all those American Blues guys in Bristol and Bath.'

'Well, I think we need to think seriously about it,' concluded Bryn, bringing the conversation to a close. 'I know we like Bath and our flat but I'm not keen on this job and I'm fed up with not having any money to spend.'

I did not remind him that we would have even less when we had a child and I stopped work. The lights of Bath glowed as we descended the hill to Lambridge and I knew we would have to make some tough decisions pretty soon.

We decided that the next time I wrote home we would request a local newspaper to suss out jobs and accommodation and Bryn started to trawl through the situations vacant in his union paper. After a few weeks he spotted a job in Evesham at The Journal Press and wrote to ask for details. Their speciality was high quality, four-colour magazine work and they had some prestigious clients. Bryn returned from the interview to explain that everything had gone well and that they could offer us some accommodation if he took the job: a three bedroomed terrace house was available.

'I'm not sure,' I said warily. 'How long have you got, to decide?'

'We could look at the house when we go up for Steve and Maggie's wedding in three weeks time. I'm sure the company will wait.' Bryn was confident and delighted that his letter-press printing skills would be valued once again.

'I'll have to leave my job at the university,' I sighed, facing up to something that had bothered me all along. 'I'd better start looking for something else.'

It was easier than I thought. I picked up a newspaper from the pile that Bryn had read through and noticed that Collins Bros, the sausage and pie factory in Evesham wanted a bacteriologist in charge of their quality control laboratory, someone who could develop tests for a range of new products.

'I'll give this a go I think. If I get an application off quickly I could have an interview when we go to look at the house.' I tried to be positive but could not help reflecting that this would mean the second time we had moved in a year. I comforted myself with the thought that I was adaptable and would enjoy making a bigger house into a home.

We drove to Redditch two days before my brother's wedding and had a reunion with my sister Jean who had arranged leave from her convent to be at the wedding. She accompanied us to Evesham the following day and we were shown round an empty house by the manager of the Journal Press. We liked what we saw and the boss confirmed that he would offer Bryn the job so they shook hands on it, there and then.

I went for my interview that afternoon and had equal success. They thought my previous experience was ideal and offered me the job. Needless to say, my parents were delighted and it helped to take away the sadness that Mum felt at her last child, her favourite one, getting married. Stephen and Margaret's wedding at St Luke's church, Headless Cross, went without a hitch and it was funny to be back in the Montville Hotel where we had had our own reception two years ago.

Steve and Margaret's Wedding, September 1967. Jean, Jim, Ann, Steve, Margaret, Dad, Mum, Maurice, Rosemary, Bryn and Angie.

Things did not continue so smoothly. We were due to move in two weeks time, but the week following our trip to Redditch I discovered that I was pregnant. Our excitement was rather overshadowed by my worry about my new job. Random thoughts flashed through my mind. Would it be fair to start a job that I would have to give up in six months time? A job that would need some settling into. A job where I would be involved in developing new products. It was the sort of position where they would expect me to stay for years. I regretted going for the interview and wished I had not accepted the job.

After lots of discussion we decided that I had better let them know immediately that I could not take up the job they had offered me and I posted off a letter the following morning feeling relieved that we could concentrate on enjoying our wonderful news about the baby.

It was time to start packing for our move in two weeks time.

Chapter 3

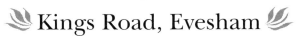 Kings Road, Evesham

T he house smelt damp as we turned the key. It was one of a dozen or so owned by the printing factory and rented to their employees but it had stood empty for a while. The red brick terraces that lined Kings Road behind their tiny front gardens had been built in the last few years of the nineteenth century when the parish of Bengeworth had expanded on the east side of the river Avon, about a mile from the centre of Evesham.

We were pleased with our new home and thought that the rent of one pound and ten shillings a week was good value. We would not be able to furnish the front lounge yet, but we could not afford to heat it so that did not matter. There was a beige-tiled fireplace in the large, rear living room and a long sash window that looked out into the back yard and we decided to put all our furniture in there. We plugged in all our electric fires to take the chill feeling off the house and went on a tour of our accommodation after the removal men had left.

The staircase struck cold, wedged into a small back lobby between the living room and kitchen. There was a draught under the back door but at least it helped to dry off the rather slimey terracotta quarry tiles. The stairs wound round three sides of the newel post to reach the landing which in turn led to three cold bedrooms and an even colder bathroom. To warm up we started to arrange the furniture that the removal men had deposited in the rooms. Our brown three-piece suite, the long teak coffee table, the two bookcases and the display cabinet full of Bryn's model soldiers all fitted in. The next day we would unpack the books and the soldiers and hang the pictures on the walls.

I was feeling rather tired and was conscious of being newly pregnant. Bryn put the kettle on and said he would walk down the road to the corner shop to see if they had any cake or buns and to buy a pint of milk. Once we had revived our flagging energy it was time to sort out the kitchen. Isolated right at the back of the house beyond the lobby it would need the paraffin stove on all day long to warm it up. Once the gas man had arrived to connect the cooker we could have the oven on with the door open; that would soon raise the temperature.

We unpacked our Midwinter china and stowed it away in the bottom of the kitchen cabinet and put our saucepans and oven-ware in the cupboard at the side of the sink. We sorted through the cardboard box of groceries that we had brought with us and stacked the tins and packets in the top of the cabinet. Tomorrow Mum and Dad would drive over from Redditch and Dad had promised to bring his electric drill so he and Bryn could fix up the white-wood cupboards on the painted brick walls.

There was a knock on the front door to herald the arrival of the gas man and he soon had our cooker fitted and working. Between us we prepared our meal; Bryn found the tin opener and worked round the metal lid of the meat-pie tin and went on to open up a tin of processed peas while I peeled the potatoes and put them on to boil.

We stuck two hot-water-bottles in our bed to air it while we slogged away unpacking clothes and cramming them into drawers.

That evening as we crouched over our electric fire we took stock of our current situation. Although Bryn's boss had promised lots of overtime we knew if we wanted to stay on target with our savings for a house I would have to find some sort of job, just for a few months. Any sort of job would do as long as it wasn't too demanding – pregnancy had made me feel vulnerable and delicate for the first time in my life. This was a new experience for me as I was usually ready to tackle anything. When the local paper came out next week I would look for a job.

We decided to keep our special news to ourselves for a few more weeks; once my parents knew we were going to start a family they would take over and start fussing.

The Journal was out and I scanned the situations vacant columns. There was something I might have a go at. The veterinary surgeons on Merstow Green wanted a kennel-maid so that afternoon I drove up town and parked in the leafy forecourt at the edge of a pleasant open space.

I stepped into the waiting room which smelt of cat pee and damp fur overlaid with disinfectant and faced the reception desk. I was quickly ushered into the boss's office.

'Have you had much experience with animals?' Mr Bowler asked me as he lounged back in his partner's chair, very much the country vet in his loud-check three-piece tweed suit and well polished brown brogues.

'Well, yes. I can ride and I've got a certificate in stable management,' I replied. 'I worked on farms for two years and dealt with cattle and pigs and studied animal health at day-release classes then at agricultural college.'

'What about small animals; cats, dogs and so forth? He continued.

'Well, we have had several cats and that's about it.'

'What about seeing blood? We wouldn't want you to faint on us during an operation. You'll be dealing with the anaesthetic; the gas and air.'

'Oh no, I'll be fine. It sounds fascinating,' I replied.

'Well you seem confident and you appear to have an ample dose of common sense. The job's yours as far as I'm concerned. I'll just have to confirm it with my wife. She's a partner but doesn't practise much these days.'

The work was going to be varied. On operating days I would have to sterilize the appropriate surgical equipment and cloths, assist with the anaesthetics and care for the animals in recovery. At surgery times I would be on hand to assist if required, lifting animals onto the examination table, holding them for injections, taking them into the kennels and mopping up any accidents. There was also a boarding kennel and cattery and I would have to take my turn on the rota with the other kennel maid to call in and feed them and clean them out at weekends. I was keen to learn and told them I would like to become a qualified veterinary nurse one day, but did not say that it wasn't likely at the moment – after all I only expected to be there for six months.

I started the job with the minimum delay and the boss introduced me.

'This is Mrs Fullard. She's our receptionist and copes with everything in the office.'

There was a crackling noise of static and a faint voice called out 'Base, come in please.'

'That's Roger Martin, our other vet calling on the RT. You'll soon learn how to use it. Our other girl must be out the back; Mrs Fullard will do the honours.'

There were difficult parts to the job as well, such as dealing with owners when their pet had been put down and worse still, taking dead animals to the council tip for burial.

After a few weeks I was just beginning to find my feet when I had a ghastly shock. It was just after lunch when I saw blood in the toilet pan and I knew that this was a sign of a potential miscarriage. Whatever should I do? I couldn't ignore it but they didn't know I was pregnant. I felt embarrassed and scared. I knew that I would have to tell someone. Mrs Fullard was on duty in the office; I would have to confide in her.

'We must let your husband know, Angela,' she said.

'I can't ring him at work. I'll have to go home and call and tell him on the way,' I whispered, almost scared to talk or move.

'I'll let the boss know when he comes in and I'll ring your doctor and tell him. You get on home.'

I took a slight diversion to reach the printing factory and burst into tears as soon as Bryn came out to see me. He told his foreman I was unwell and escorted me home and I was soon lowering myself carefully into bed. The next day, at ten weeks pregnant, we lost our baby. Bryn went down to the phone box to ring my parents and they soon drove over to visit me feeling rather aggrieved that we had not told them we were going to start a family.

A week later after a short stay in hospital and warnings that I must not conceive for at least six months I was back at work at the vets, and luckily the busy practice and the need to learn so many new things helped me to get over the trauma of the miscarriage.

It was almost Christmas and we did the rounds of the family. My sister Rosemary and her husband were both excellent at playing the host and visitors were always assured of a warm welcome. It was nice to see their children including my god-daughter Susan.

Steve and Margaret were renting a house in Redditch and looking forward to moving out to a new house in Inkberrow. We usually met up with them at Mum and Dad's, but my brother was not yet twenty and I felt old and worldly-wise when we saw them.

Jean was still in the convent at Laleham Abbey and of course we rarely saw her. My eldest brother Jim was a Chief Petty Officer in the submarine division of the Royal Navy and when he wasn't away on exercises he was based at Portsmouth where he lived with his wife and two children. He was due for a period of service in Singapore and was shortly to move there with his family.

Mum would feed us with tit-bits of news and gradually we would build up a picture of what everybody was doing. Grandad Winnett had died in May

1967 just one month before he and Gran were due to celebrate their diamond wedding anniversary. He had developed symptoms of senility and Mum told a story of him viciously poking the coal-effect electric fire with his walking stick to stir up a blaze and ramming it right through the plastic. As his symptoms progressed his vagueness calmed his temper somewhat. Now we were living nearer we were able to visit Granny Winnett and she always appreciated seeing us.

For the next few months I became Mrs Conventional. I went to work five days a week; I did my dusting, polished my windows and cleaned my cooker, and I transferred my membership of the Methodist church from Bradford on Avon to Evesham and started to go to church again on Sunday morning. We visited my parents on a regular basis and kept abreast of family happenings. I was soon bored rigid.

My work was alright: it was unusual enough to satisfy me. I helped with operations as diverse as cleaning cat's teeth to pinning dog's hip bones, from delicate eye operations to puncturing the rumen of a cow with bloat, out in a field. Mr Bowler would bring me the operating list the evening before.

'We've six tomorrow, Angela. Get the instruments and cloths boiled up for these. We'll start promptly at nine. Are all the animals in overnight?'

'Just the cat to come in when the surgery opens in the morning,' I replied.

At eight-thirty I would have the stainless steel sterilizers boiling on the gas ring. I had selected the surgical equipment from the lists required for each technique and chosen the relevant green cloth with a hemmed slit in it to correspond with the size of the incision. Just before nine o'clock I would drain off the water but keep the lid firmly in place while the shining pans were lined up in order in the preparation room ready to be transferred to the operating theatre. I would bring the first animal in and lift it onto the table and hold its paw ready for the vet to inject the anaesthetic as the smell of surgical spirit filled the room.

In the evening I wanted to relive with Bryn the details of the operations and the veterinary surgeon's skill, but usually he got in first and regaled me with step-by-step stories of difficult print jobs or complained of the tedium of long print runs.

On alternate weekends I took my turn to clean out and feed the boarding animals. The cats were kept in a loft above the ramshackle buildings that joined the surgery. The pens were arranged in rows and once I had renewed the paper bedding, allocated their water or milk and spooned out their food I loved to give the cats a bit of TLC and stroked them until they purred. Although many of the owners supplied a cat's special piece of blanket or left tins of their favourite food I knew the moggies would be missing their owners.

On the outskirts of town along the Worcester Road and approached up a long, bumpy track were the boarding kennels. A central passage gave access to about ten runs on each side and strong wire mesh topped the solid partitions. As soon as I drove up the track and parked the Transit van outside a deafening cacophony of barking would ensue. As I un-padlocked the doors the dogs would gradually fall silent knowing that they would soon be fed. I mucked them out and hosed down the runs then cut up the solid blocks of dog meat ready to dollop it into the stainless steel bowls. The dogs had clean, well ventilated accommodation but it wasn't like hearing their owners call 'Walkies'. Each day I would make time to walk two or three of liveliest animals between the hazel and wild plum trees along the track. The kennels were situated just outside the garden of a huge ancient house that looked like an old manor. The dipping gabled roof was all shapes and the windows and doors looked centuries old. Sometimes an occupant would call across and offer me a mug of tea or a glass of water and from what I could glean they were a big family and glad of their tenancy.

We still found time for most of our hobbies. Winter evenings for Bryn meant converting and painting model soldiers or reading reference books. I would draw the curtains and switch on the standard lamp and then I might be involved in a complicated sewing project cutting out a shirt with twenty pattern pieces or struggling with four knitting pins to make a fair-isle beret. Pulsing away in the background would always be jazz and I learnt to recognise the styles of the great names like Art Tatum, Dizzy Gillespie, Miles Davis and Charlie Parker. Bryn would keep abreast of all the latest happenings in the music world by reading *Jazz Journal* and *Jazz Monthly* and each week he would pick up a copy of *The New Musical Express* and *Melody Maker*.

I still read avidly and I soon devoured Iris Murdoch's new book *The Italian Girl* and I bought Jane Gaskells science fiction trilogy based on the city of *Atlan*. Also during 1967 I discovered Doris Lessing's thought-provoking political novel *Landlocked*.

My collection of non-fiction books was growing too. For my birthday in May Bryn had bought me the Rev Keble-Martin's *Concise British Flora* illustrated with wonderful hand-painted colour plates of all the native plants of Britain and very informative text. I absorbed the information and looked for samples of plants to identify and press in Bryn's old wooden tie-press. I spread the flowers out on blotting paper then screwed them down in the press which had never been used for ties since it was given as his twenty-first birthday present.

My other birthday present was the weighty *Shell Guide to Britain,* divided into counties and illustrated with photos and colour plates of paintings of the countryside specially commissioned. I pored over the entries reinforcing details of places I already knew – Worcestershire, Warwickshire, Devon and Wiltshire and making notes about places that I hoped we would soon be able to visit – Cornwall and the whole of Wales.

I soon became bored with my routine of work followed by housework and we renewed our habit of going out for the day on Saturdays. Our old Ford Popular served us well. I drove us to either Cheltenham, Stratford upon Avon or Worcester or if we wanted to go further afield we would venture to Gloucester, Oxford or Birmingham to do our shopping and browse the book and record shops, the museums and galleries and explore the back streets.

We spent Christmas in Torquay visiting Bryn's family and noticed immediately that Mr Jenkins' health had deteriorated. He had had to give up work now as the premature senility progressed and Bryn's Mum was finding it rather a strain looking after him as he had a tendency to wander off when they were out shopping. Over the holiday period I read my new book *Tarka the Otter* and thought how wonderful it would be to visit north Devon where the book was set.

Hello Goodbye by the Beatles was in the charts for seven weeks around Christmas and we were pleased to say goodbye to 1967 and hello to 1968.

* * * * *

Things were going better for us now. Bryn was earning £15 a week plus overtime and my wages were about £11. We were not only able to continue saving for the deposit on our house but could afford some new clothes. I chose a dark navy, double-breasted coat that fitted at the waist and featured a detachable cape that came down to my elbows. The coat and cape were lined with a glorious turquoise blue silk. I accessorised it with a huge black handbag and chunky, black, soft leather shoes with a huge tongue that came up my ankles. My winter dress was soft black wool with tightly-buttoned, gathered cuffs and the shortest of skirts. Bryn had black needle-cord trousers and pale cream, suede ankle boots that looked very striking with his long, black leather coat.

In the spring I added two slinky nylon dresses to my wardrobe. One was scarlet with a huge white tab collar and the other was pure white and I thought it looked good teamed with a coloured scarf. Bryn and I adored each other and loved to go out together looking good. Our personalities seemed to complement each other and our interests were diverse enough not to go stale but similar enough to share common experiences. We were inseparable and preferred each other's company to anyone else's.

We still saw my family and in June decided to go for a few days holiday in Wales with Steve and Margaret. We got on very well as we explored Snowdonia and Harlech.

When we returned to Evesham Bryn and I had a serious talk. After my miscarriage I had been prescribed the contraceptive pill but now we decided that it was time to try for another baby. Within weeks of our decision I realised I was pregnant and we went to Redditch to tell my parents.

'Baby? You're having a baby? After what happened?' spluttered my mother incredulously.

'They said it would be alright to try after six months, Mum. I know I won't be in the clear until I pass the twelve-week danger period but you don't sound very pleased!'

'No! You're right! In fact I am very surprised. You are too selfish to have a child; you're so wrapped up in each other I wonder how you will be able to manage.'

I felt deflated and disappointed. I thought congratulations might be in order. Dad gave me a reassuring squeeze on the arm.

'Take care of yourself, ducky. You don't want anything to happen this time.'

We needed time on our own to come to terms with our exciting news and decided to go to Cornwall for a week's holiday. For my birthday Bryn had bought me Daphne du Maurier's *Vanishing Cornwall* in which she describes the romantic heritage of Cornwall. She tells of the customs, legends and superstitions, of the gentry and the tin-miners and of the eccentrics and the clerics. I had absorbed the book word by word and fired Bryn's enthusiasm. Now we wanted to explore the county for ourselves. We made an itinerary to cover as many as possible of the sites in the book.

We set off on our five-day break with a night at Bryn's mother's our first destination. All the way down to Devon we talked about the child we expected. Our love for our child would know no bounds. It would be a combination of all we admired in each other; sensitive and caring, practical and daring. Our child would be honest and true, brave and strong. As parents we would be fair but firm, we would love it but not spoil him or her.

Our child would know right from wrong; we would show it by our example. We would encourage our child to know the wonders of nature, the miracles of science and the magic of history. It would not matter whether it was a daughter or a son, we would visit museums and galleries, castles and concerts. We hoped our child would be artistic and musical, and would devour books as we did ourselves. We didn't tire of the subject; we were part of the most wonderful thing in the world – creation.

We had decided on names even before we knew we were starting a family. If it was a boy he would be called Dylan after the talented and charismatic poet Dylan Thomas and following in the Welsh tradition of the Jenkins family – Bryn's father was named Morgan. Robert Zimmerman had also reinvented himself as Bob Dylan in honour of the poet. If we had a girl she would be called Meryl a Welsh version of Mary, my mother's name.

Our holiday was marvellous and everything we hoped it would be. Sunday morning dawned warm and misty and after an early breakfast we lugged our bags down the steps from the flat at Stantaway House and slung them in the car that I had parked half on the stony track and half in the blackberry bushes. Our route took us along the familiar road to Newton Abbot, relatively free of traffic on a Sunday morning. We left Newton on the Ashburton Road and as we left the houses behind I glanced across at Seale-Hayne, the agricultural college where I had gained my Diploma in Dairying. We motored along the A38 towards Ashburton and turned into the ancient town to take the road up over Dartmoor. I launched our old car at the steep gradient of Holme Chase and the engine ground its way round the hairpin bend up to the summit. Once we had moved out of the canopy of trees and were up on the moor the brilliant sun sparkled in the azure sky. Kestrels hung motionless in the air ready to strike unsuspecting rabbits and butterflies hovered above the golden gorse blossom. Huge granite outcrops dotted the sheep-grazed moorland giving the landscape a wild, bleak look.

We had a lot of ground to cover and as we approached Princetown we only had time to comment on the austere granite walls of Dartmoor prison built in Napoleonic times and to wonder if we would see any gangs of prisoners. We were on the downhill run towards Tavistock now and we thought the town looked interesting and made up our minds to return one day.

On up the other side of the valley we drove across the last few lumps and bumps of Devon then we crossed the River Tamar and we were in the county of Cornwall. Did I imagine it? Did it seem different from Devon? Surely the atmosphere had changed. Perhaps I was being fanciful; perhaps I had absorbed too much of Daphne du Maurier.

Launceston's wonderful Norman castle loomed up against the skyline, its stone keep sitting on top of a pimple of an earth motte. The jumble of town lay sprawling at its feet. We parked the car and wandered round until we found a bakery and bought two lardy cakes to finish off our home made sandwiches. We were two thirds of the way to Tintagel and we wanted to arrive in plenty of time to explore and find a B&B.

As we drove on I could feel the sense of anticipation mounting. We were going to visit one of the most mystical of Cornwall's sites, a place of myth and legend, the birthplace of King Arthur. I parked the car at the top of the town and we walked down the village street, already busy with tourists on this August day.

We descended the stony track towards the castle. A huge headland almost formed an island separated by only a narrow isthmus with the sea pounding on each side of a sheer drop. Celtic monks had settled there in the sixth century on the site of the Iron Age hill fort five hundred years before the Normans built their castle on the precipitous slopes. I sat on a stone wall, the on-shore wind blowing against my back and tried to shut out the other day-trippers while I absorbed the atmosphere and cast my eyes across wild sweeps of cliff and wind blown turf to the outlines of the monk's cells on the rocky outcrops. As the sea mist rolled in and the sun started to set we knew it was time to find some accommodation for the night so we walked slowly back up the track and through the village to our car.

We had a long drive ahead of us on Monday. Naturally we wanted to see as much as possible on this whistle-stop tour and had decided to get down to Land's End. We motored down to Wadebridge and St Columb Major knowing we couldn't do justice to all the scenic places on the coast and told ourselves that there would be other holidays in which to explore Padstow, Trevose and Bedruthan Steps. We were desperate for a closer view of the Atlantic Ocean and turned towards Newquay.

As we drove down the long stretch of Watergate Bay into the town dominated by guest houses and huge hotels we decided to make for the famous Fistral Bay to watch the mighty rollers break onto the shore. Later we walked on the headland past the Huer's House when years ago a lookout had scanned the sea for shoals of pilchards.

We needed another day to reach Lands End; there was so much to see on the way. We wanted to visit the mine buildings on St Agnes head standing sheer above the sea before driving down the rocky spine if western Cornwall to Lands End. Bryn had *Vanishing Cornwall* balanced on his lap while he leafed through the *Shell Guide to Britain* anxious that we didn't miss any of the scenic delights or mysterious locations that had fuelled our imagination.

St Ives looked wonderful but we knew we hadn't time to absorb the essence of the artists' colony and many galleries. Instead we chose to make for the mystical Lanyon Quiot the eroded burial chamber of a Stone Age long barrow and as we reached up our hands to touch the pitted granite slab stone a wicked wind whistled across the moorland.

Lands End was an anti-climax and we drove round the toe of the county to Lamorna and Mousehole before motoring via Newlyn to Penzance and Marazion to view St Michael's Mount given by Edward the Confessor to the monks of Mont St Michel in Brittany.

Our holiday was almost over and we were conscious that the last couple of days would be rushed as we drove along the south coast back to Torquay. Helston, Falmouth and Truro were a blur but we made time to climb Roche Rock to the ruined hermit's cell built into the unfriendly local stone of this bleak outcrop in the middle of the china clay district just outside St Austell. On to Fowey where we desperately wanted to park the car and explore this cramped and romantic town but we decided to abandon a detailed investigation and catch the Bodinnick Ferry to Looe and St Germans and so to Saltash and the A38.

We returned to work with our heads full of Polperro and Penrose, Malpas and Madron. A few weeks later I thought I should tell my employers that I was pregnant.

'Well Angela, I think it would be better for all concerned if you gave up work now. You don't want to risk another miscarriage do you?'

It wasn't the response I had expected. I had hoped to get a few more pay packets before I gave up.

'Er, I suppose so,' I agreed doubtfully. 'Will it affect my maternity grant or allowance?' I queried.

'You'd better find out. We should be able to square it. Say it was due to ill health.'

So it was decided. In some ways I was not sorry; I certainly did not want to risk another miscarriage but on the other hand I felt so well and hoped that I was going to sail through my pregnancy.

In September we had the chance to visit London for a few days, staying with Bryn's uncle Trevor in Victoria. By the time we came back I knew I was safe, I had passed the critical danger period. Our busy itinerary passed in something of a blur as we crossed off London Zoo, Soho, Horse Guards Parade and the store of Liberty and Co.

Angie, Soho Square, London, September 1968.

Once back in Evesham I had time on my hands now. We decided to decorate our smallest bedroom as a nursery and chose a clear primrose yellow colour. Bryn sanded down a second-hand cot we had been given and gave it a coat of jolly orange paint and then used the same colour on the drawers of the big old chest Dad had bought us when we were engaged. I made gingham curtains to match and suddenly the room was transformed.

I decided to make some cot sheets out of old bed linen; I couldn't see the point of spending money on anything I could recycle. I embellished the top edge of stitching with coloured braid to go with the nursery then moved on to making the pram sheets as well. Each finished item was carefully stowed in the big bottom drawer of the chest to await the new arrival.

Next I put my craft skills to use and began a patchwork pram quilt. I'd never made one before and read a book about the technique. Granny Winnett and Auntie Chris turned out several old skirts, dresses and blouses for me to cut into hexagonal pieces and I added to these by raiding my fabric remnants. Slowly the quilt began to grow as I sewed the patches together.

'How big will it be?' queried Bryn.

'We'll have to check the size of a pram in the Mothercare catalogue,' I guessed. 'We want to have a look at them anyway to get an idea of the prices.'

Once the pram cover was finished I thought it would be a challenge to try to make a jointed teddy bear. I had seen a pattern in the craft shop in Stratford upon Avon and they sold a range of safe fur fabric as well. The kit came complete with wooden discs to go inside the limbs at the joints, all the pattern pieces and the eyes and their safety fasteners. We chose a soft toffee-brown fur and some delicate suede for the bear's pads. After a couple of weeks the skin of the teddy was finished and then I had to give him some character by stuffing him with kapok. When he was complete we sat him on the chair in the nursery to await the arrival of his owner.

My bump was starting to show and my clothes were getting tight so I made three sleeveless maternity dresses to see me through the next four months, choosing the colours to co-ordinate with my blouses and polo-necked jumpers.

My nesting instincts were at fever-pitch and once I had finished *my* clothes I wondered if I could make any clothes for the expected arrival. Mum, Granny and Auntie were all busy knitting matinee jackets, bootees and mittens so I knew the baby would be well stocked in this department. I searched through the pattern books at Hamilton and Bell's department store in the High Street and saw adorable dresses that could be quickly adjusted to romper suits by the addition of a gusset. The bodice of the garment was smocked in the traditional way with coloured silks. Through a client at work I had heard of an elderly woman who was a talented smocker and contacted her to ask if she would teach me the skill. A couple of weeks later I called at her house with my yellow squared fabric, pins, needles and embroidery silks. She showed me how to gather the fabric up on a thread and hold it in place on a frame. It would hang in minute creases ready to be smocked into permanent pleats. She explained that three different stitches in two or three colours would be fine for a child's garment and I tentatively began the first row.

I went home with a sketch plan of the frame, which was merely two notched dowels fixed upright each end of a heavy slab of wood. Even Bryn with his limited carpentry skills could make that and I soon had my fabric hanging from my own smocking frame. A month later I had three outfits ready for the finishing touch – if we had a girl I would do a neat hem on the skirt, if we had a boy I would sew in the gusset and gather the leg-holes with some elastic.

As the time moved closer we started to visit Mothercare and bought various bits and pieces we thought we would need. Mum assured me that relatives and friends would want to give us things as presents and suggested we only chose the more utilitarian items.

My doctor said that it was time to consider ante-natal classes and made a note of the time and place. Since living in Evesham we hadn't had much chance to explore the rather pretty town and the walk to the clinic would give me the opportunity. The sessions were held in the Welfare Clinic at the entrance to Avonside Hospital and I presented myself there feeling very conspicuous and faintly embarrassed. The helpers soon reassured me and within five minutes I was lying on the floor learning breathing exercises.

Over the next three months I was guided through the stages of pregnancy and child birth with the help of charts and models. The nurses confirmed my belief that having a baby was the most natural thing in the world but help would be at hand if it was needed. As my pregnancy developed I felt the classic example of an expectant mother; I was glowing, my skin was good, my hair shone and my excitement showed in my eyes. There was a down-side of course – my ankles swelled up, I put on too much weight and new stretch-marks appeared every day!

My walks to and from the ante-natal clinic became a source of delight and at the weekend I would enjoy showing Bryn the new places I had discovered.

Evesham was founded at a strategic position in a loop on the river Avon and lies in a wide vale between the Cotswold and Malvern Hills. It is a delightful market town with a wide tree-lined High Street and a pleasant mix of building styles dating from the twelfth-century All Saints Church through the Tudor and Georgian periods to Victorian terraces. I loved wandering along the lime-lined riverside walk, under the huge whale's jaw bone as I made my way to the clinic. As I became more familiar with the layout of the town I ventured down backstreets and along linking paths and tracks.

'I want you to see the Abbey Park and Bell Tower,' I told Bryn one Sunday morning. 'You'll love it – there are few masonry remains of an old wall that could be part of the cloisters or something,' I enthused.

'Shall I pack my sketchbook?' Bryn queried. 'I may have a chance to get something down on paper.'

'Maybe,' I replied hesitantly. 'Don't forget I am finding it a bit more difficult to sit on anything uncomfortable. It may be better if I just keep walking slowly. Anyway, it's a bit chilly isn't it?'

We set off in the watery winter sun, taking a short cut down to Port Street and following the narrow road down to the river bridge passing the shops that were now becoming familiar: the opticians, the camera shop and Hampton's the newsagents and sweet shop.

We reached the River Avon and leaned over the stone parapet to look for swans gliding down the placid water then started our ascent of Bridge Street ignoring two possible entrances to the Abbey Park. The first was down the drive next to the Marine Ballroom situated on the river bank and the next was under the arch of the four-hundred-year-old Crown Hotel, an old coaching inn which was on the route from Birmingham to Cheltenham. We wanted to walk past the magnificent half-timbered fifteenth century Booth Hall and into the market square. From there we could pass under Abbot Reginald's Gateway into the churchyard.

'I've been reading about all this in a library book,' I showed off to Bryn. 'If you go that way you come to the Almonry which is now the museum and if you turn left you walk under the Bell Tower.'

We had often heard the bells ring out tunes from the huge detached campanile and would soon be walking underneath the pinnacled structure built by Abbot Clement Lichfield but first we wandered between the two churches of All Saints and St Lawrence.

'I think I've got this right,' I pondered. 'One church was built for the townspeople and one to accommodate the pilgrims who came to worship the shrines at the abbey. Legend has it that the Benedictine abbey was founded on the spot where a swineherd had a vision of the Virgin Mary.' I had exhausted my stock of information now, and under the bell tower we turned right following the old wall to look at a ruined arch.

I needed five minutes rest so we perched on a bench near the swing-park and admired the view down the slope over the boating lake and paddling pond towards the river. We had spent enough time on our exploration of the town and it was time to turn for home where the thoughts of a mug of tea and toasted pikelets suddenly seemed very appealing. Bryn and I walked past the old stables of The Crown and under the brick-paved archway where the stage coach would have drawn up and then we re-entered Bridge Street to make our way back to Kings Road.

That evening Bryn wrote one of his delightful rambling letters to his Mum, telling her all about our walk. It was only a short time since our Christmas visit but she had been feeling rather low in spirits since Mr Jenkins had been admitted into residential care at the Exvale Hospital, near Exeter, miles away. She had no longer been able to care for him at home as his illness had quickly progressed but Bryn knew her relief regarding his hospitalisation was inevitably tinged with sadness and loneliness. Bryn's detailed epistles were the next best thing to a visit and Mrs Jenkins absorbed every phrase of his wordy descriptions of our life in Evesham.

My parents too were feeling low and found it hard to come to terms with the worst news of 1968. My brother Jim, stationed with his wife and two sons at the Royal Navy submarine base in Singapore had had a fatal accident. They just couldn't believe the phone call they had received. He had been travelling home from the base to his quarters when a tropical storm had obscured his vision and he had collided with a tree. Mum and Dad kept going over the ghastly details and longed for first hand information from his wife Ann. It was weeks later when she arrived back in the UK and my parents went to meet her and the boys to share their grief. They were all so proud of Jim, who was hoping to be commissioned as a lieutenant in the Royal Navy. They tried to protect me from the worst of the sorrow as they feared the news would have an adverse affect on my pregnancy. Inevitably I cast my mind back to my childhood and the excitement of Jim's visits on leave when he would bring back gifts from abroad such as a Maltese lace tablecloth for Mum and a chunk of stalactite from the caves in the Rock of Gibraltar for me. He had told us tales of foreign countries, and sent me post cards from around the world and piles of exotic coins and stamps. It was only eight years since I had proudly acted as bridesmaid at his and Ann's wedding.

The weeks passed quickly to my expected date of confinement. I hoped that my pregnancy would help to improve my relationship with Mum and draw us closer together. We had never really seen eye to eye and there was often a feeling of antagonism, almost bitterness from her. I often mused on it: Mum seemed to carry resentment and regret, but I wasn't sure what it was about. Of course, by now I knew a little of her early life but she never talked openly about it. My relationship with Dad was as close as ever and sometimes I wondered if Mum was jealous of the open affection he showed for me.

* * * * *

I passed my due date and was admitted to Avonside Maternity Hospital a week later. On Thursday 3rd April at six-fifteen in the morning I gave birth to our son Dylan who weighed in at nine pounds and two ounces. Bryn rang the hospital from the call-box on his way to work and was told the news. He was soon there beside me and we gazed in amazement at our beautiful baby with his fine down of fair hair and perfectly shaped head lying peacefully in the crib beside my bed.

At tea-time Mum and Dad arrived with a camera but were only allowed to take one photograph of our son, Dylan. The babies were taken away and put in the nursery down the corridor except during feeding time so we had little time to nurse and cuddle our newborn infant. Mum was relieved that I had decided to bottle-feed – 'so much better my dear. You would be so restricted if you nursed him (Mum's euphemism for breast-feeding), you wouldn't be able to go out.' She said they had a car full of presents and they would take them back to the house ready for our homecoming and I soon forgot the difficult time I had been through.

Ten days later and with one session's experience of changing a nappy, and written instructions on how to mix a feed of dried milk I was waved off in a taxi, sitting in the back with Dylan, while Bryn sat up-front to direct the driver.

The next day I was on my own; Bryn had to go back to work and even if she had been able to come, I didn't want Mum taking over. I enjoyed the learning process and the closeness and soon felt confident at feeding, changing and bathing our son. I loved singing to him and would rock him to the beat of the tunes; I would play the radio or a record and walk round the room half dancing with Dylan in my arms. Bryn was besotted with him and had difficulty realising that he was ours; our creation; our responsibility. We decided that as far as possible we would still go to all the same places as before – we would just take the pram or carry-cot or pushchair and Dylan would come too. Eight weeks after he was born we made our usual Whitsun trip to Torquay and introduced our baby to his other grandmother and took him round to see aunts and uncles and friends.

Bryn, Angie and Dylan May 1969. Stantaway House.

In September we went to Stratford on Avon Mop Fair and Dylan seemed entranced at the bright lights, the roundabouts and the galloping horses. We went on outings to Winchcombe, to Stow-on-the-Wold and to Bourton-on-the-Water. Back home everyone wanted to see him. Mum and Dad couldn't get enough of him and my father in particular seemed very proud of his new grandson. I took him regularly to visit Granny Winnett who would jiggle him on her lap and walk round the garden showing him the flowers.

Our life seemed everything we wanted it to be. Soon however a few cracks appeared in the veneer of happiness.

For one thing, money was short and Mum didn't help by quoting 'when poverty comes in through the door, love flies out of the window.' I felt we could manage on Bryn's pay providing we made a few economies. There was very little to economise on in the household budget: we used paraffin stoves to supplement expensive electric heating, I sewed and knitted lots of our clothes and we ate very cheaply.

Each week I would try to enlarge our range of meals. I enjoyed cooking and making the most of the ingredients we had in the pantry under the stairs but to fill us up and provide a nourishing diet seemed a challenge. Sunday almost always meant roast chicken and all the trimmings and Monday was chicken casserole with potatoes, onions, carrots and tinned tomatoes added to the pot, and chives cut from the garden. The other days I would cook sausages, or meat pies in a tin, or maybe luncheon-meat fritters with the block of meat cut in eight slices and deep-fried in a coating of batter. I would make liver and onion casserole with a dusting of flour on the liver slices thickening up the tasty onion gravy and potatoes done to a soft texture by several hours in the old brown crock-pot passed on to me by Granny. Bryn enjoyed my version of risotto although we didn't call it that. I would cook a chopped onion in a dollop of fat and add half a pound of minced beef. Once it was browned I added a tin of tomatoes and two or three handfuls of rice and covered it with a dissolved Oxo cube and boiling water. After forty-five minutes the stock would be absorbed and the rice swollen up. Sometimes I gave it an extra flavour with a dollop of brown sauce and I felt this meal was one of my triumphs! It was easy to make, needed very little attention, was filling and tasty and best of all it was cheap!

No! I didn't think I could economise on any aspect of housekeeping. It would have to be leisure – but we hardly went out except on jaunts in the car. I decided to broach another subject with Bryn.

'What about cutting down on papers and magazines?' I said in a nonchalant voice one Sunday morning when Bryn had his head in the review section of the Sunday Times.

'What? You mean stop having a Sunday paper?' he countered incredulously. 'As it is all I do is *read* about concerts and jazz gigs and books!'

'That's not true,' I replied quickly. 'You still buy records: one almost every week, but that's not what I'm talking about. Three-quarters of the paper never gets read; between us we read the review and the colour magazine and I wrap the potato peelings in the rest.'

'Well, I'm not giving up one of my few pleasures,' he emphasised.

I failed to recognise when to stop and continued,

'What about a couple of mags then? You have Jazz Monthly and Jazz Journal and then there's the NME and Melody Maker.'

'For goodness sake, stop getting at me and shut up!' he snapped back. 'I work all week and put in hours of overtime and if I can't buy a few magazines and papers it's a poor thing!'

It was time to close the subject for now but I mused that it was Bryn who complained about lack of spending money, not me. Already we were beginning to miss my pay-packet and I thought I would have to do something about it.

When I had pushed Dylan up through the town in his pram to visit my former colleagues at the veterinary surgery they told me that the staff in the office next door would like to see him. It was the local Careers Office and they had always said hello when they saw me going to my lunch-break. The senior officer admired my lovely baby and then paused a moment while she seemed to be considering something.

'I don't suppose you would be interested in helping me out at home a couple of mornings a week?' she asked tentatively. 'Although I live on my own I don't have much opportunity for housework with such a demanding job and meetings to go to in the evenings.'

Here it seemed, could be the answer to some of our financial difficulties. I arranged to visit her house at Owlets End and once I saw the lovely sprawling Edwardian-style house set in a pretty garden I readily agreed.

'You could put your baby in his pram underneath the apple trees,' she explained. 'I wouldn't mind at all if you had to stop occasionally to see to him'

We walked round the house talking through the work schedule. I would clean upstairs one morning and downstairs on the other. I could polish the furniture and clean the windows on a rota and she would leave me a note if there was anything else.

'You could make your coffee and sit in the day room to drink it; I could leave a magazine for you to read. Would a fifteen minute break be alright?'

I readily agreed to the pay: it would take our combined pay-packets up to over twenty pounds a week. I arranged to start work on the next Tuesday and I always looked forward to the four hours a week I spent working in this spacious house. Dylan would kick contentedly under a cat-net in his pram in the garden while I got on with my cleaning.

At home I organised my housework in traditional style. Every morning after clearing up breakfast and sterilising Dylan's bottle in the plastic Milton bath I would wash the nappies, hauling them, one by one out of the lidded bucket where they had been soaking in the sanitising fluid and hand-washing them in the big stainless steel sink. If the weather was too wet to peg them out I would drape them over the bars in the enamelled Flatley electric drying-cabinet wedged into a corner of the kitchen. The warmth helped to take the cold edge off the kitchen and it would be nice for Dylan's bath. By following a strict routine I fitted my washing and housework into the time before lunch. I could do shopping after I'd done my cleaning job or when I'd been to the Welfare Clinic and the ironing while Dylan was having his afternoon nap.

* * * * *

While we were indulging ourselves completely in the pleasure of being parents life continued for the rest of the family.

Mum and Dad were doing well now they didn't have any children left at home. Mum was working in the Department of Social Security offices on the pensions section and thoroughly enjoyed her job as a clerical assistant. Sometimes she acted-up as a clerical officer and the added responsibility attracted a higher pay rate. She had made many new friends in the office and she looked both attractive and confident. Her iron-grey hair was coiled on top of her head in a loose bun and her clear unwrinkled skin glowed healthily. She was slim and stood two or three inches taller than me. When away from the office Mum favoured slacks teamed with a black or navy jumper but one day she surprised us by buying an orange jersey-wool trouser suit and she looked stunning.

Dad had started to put on weight: he was almost sixty-five and wasn't so active – at work or at home. He now worked as a maintenance electrician at Abel Morrell's needle factory. It was still shift work but he could take things a little easier when not called on to fix a problem. He still had a good head of wavy hair – almost white now but his calm, affable manner and interest in everything practical and intellectual made him seem young.

Mum and Dad were able to socialise more and held supper-parties where the sherry and gin would flow and they would play pontoon for sixpences. Mum loved being hostess; she always provided a good supper of cocktail sausages, slices of pork pie, ham sandwiches, cheese and pineapple on sticks and bowls of salty biscuits. Her speciality was thinly sliced cucumber soaked overnight in a dish of vinegar and for some reason my parents' friends thought that this was very sophisticated! They would stack records up on the Garrard auto-change deck and the party would be in full swing until the small hours.

My parents would have liked to move to a house in the nearby countryside and take on a renovation project. Over the years they had looked at several houses – Traceybourne at Morton Bagot, the old station at Kings Coughton, the ruined windmill in a quarry at Inkberrow and the caretaker's house next to Cookhill Baptist Church but as they grew older they realised it would be impractical and they would miss their friends and the home they had made in Redditch. Mum and Dad had worked long and hard on making a beautiful home. Mum still tackled upholstery jobs on chairs and stools and had learnt how to make stylish silk lampshades with co-ordinating trimmings. Dad had turned out wrought-iron table lamps, coffee tables, and magazine racks from the bench in his workshop as well as renovating antique furniture and when they were teamed with Mum's offerings and set against her sophisticated colour schemes the house had a unique glamour. The rooms would be topped off by wonderful flower arrangements, usually picked from the garden of number forty-five. Mum would deftly and intuitively poke the stalks into one of her beautiful vases, grading the flowers for colour and height without stopping until she stood back to consider her work of art. On a rare day off they would drive to The Neville or The Green Dragon or sometimes to The Why Not on The

Ridgeway where decades before, Grandad used to go in for a pint and leave Granny outside on the bench under the window with Mum as a little girl. Gran would sip her stout while Mum enjoyed a glass of lemonade.

I had hoped that once I had a child of my own it would bring me and Mum closer together, especially after her own mother had died in September 1969. Mum was heartbroken when she heard of her mother's death. She had admired her all her life and often talked of both her physical strength and practical abilities, and of her inner moral strength. I loved my dear Granny too and remembered with affection all the times I had spent with her absorbing her calm wisdom.

Mum and I had never seemed to develop that closeness. She seemed cold and distant sometimes. If I tried to give her a hug she seemed tense and would back off. She appeared scared to show physical closeness; even with Dad they were not overtly affectionate – sometimes they would link arms or briefly twine their arms around each other's waist but that was it. Mum became embarrassed if Bryn and I showed affection to each other and would say 'come on, stop that now.' She was a woman of strong emotions: that could not be in doubt – she loved, hated, showed envy and fear but they were kept in check; denied; and rarely manifested themselves in a physical way.

She was a woman to whom duty was everything; she had learnt at her mother's knee. Duty to care for her first husband who was frequently cruel, duty to care for ungrateful cantankerous ageing relatives, duty to remember the dead and keep their graves tidy and duty to put yourself last in all things. My mother learnt a life of self-denial and sacrifice. I could never, ever be grateful enough for the sacrifices that had been made for *me*. They were listed over and over again; it seemed to me that love was conditional. I couldn't be loved for myself.

I would lie in bed some nights, restless, thinking about a recent visit to Mum. What exactly did she want from me? She showed her disapproval in so many ways – by looks, body-language and words.

I decided to write her a letter: I listed all the things that might not be approved of – if they were true! I wasn't having an extra-marital affair, I didn't have criminal tendencies, I didn't lie or cheat, I had a heterosexual relationship, I didn't owe money; the list went on… but I didn't post it. I could not face the outcome; a family row; an inquest about my feelings; the denial that anything was wrong. Instead I made a decision to try to do things to please her whilst not compromising my own personality and beliefs. It was an uphill struggle. Mum had a strong work ethic; you worked until you dropped. Jobs didn't get done by not doing them. Enthusiasm starts the race and perseverance ends it. Don't put off until tomorrow what you can do today. Mum's favourite sayings rang in my ears and with her as a role-model I learnt to feel guilty if I hadn't managed to finish my tasks for the day and cross everything off my list.

It didn't work: I still knew that I didn't have her approval and she showed it. She hinted that I did not do my housework right, that I fussed over our baby and spoilt him, that my clothes were inappropriate for a married woman and that I was too extrovert and boisterous. I talked it over with Bryn; I couldn't take much more, I had taken on the roles of housewife, mother, painter and decorator, gardener and part-time worker but I still didn't seem to be the daughter my mother wanted.

I thought back over the bare details I knew of my mother's early life: her marriage to an older man to get away from the family house where she was ill-treated by her father and picked on by her sisters; her unhappy first marriage where she suffered abuse. Were these the reasons that our mother-daughter relationship had never blossomed, why she was so critical?

Was I being pathetic? Too sensitive? I didn't think so and Bryn backed me up. By the time Dylan was one year old in the spring of 1970 we decided to move house and put a bit more distance between us and my parents. I was under pressure all the time: to do my housework in a particular way; to adjust Dylan's routine, to be more rigid. Motherhood wasn't an easy job and I wanted to be good at it but I was beginning to feel guilty, to wonder if I was doing things right. Bryn was in complete agreement; he too had never felt approval from my parents. Strangely, once we had decided to move things seemed better between me and Mum: not that we had told my parents yet – that could wait a while – but I didn't feel so tense, on trial, guilty. Maybe that was because we knew that once we had moved we would be too far away for criticism or maybe my mother was at last seeing me in a different light. We had some happy times together visiting Redditch with Dylan especially when everyone was relaxed and the barriers were down. There were still opportunities for a black look such as when we went to Mum's birthday each wearing our new outfits. Bryn had a red and yellow kaftan-type tunic with a fringed hem which he wore with skin-tight Donegal tweed trousers and cuban-heeled boots. It was inevitable that he received an incredulous stare before Mum's eyes were riveted to my mini-skirt showing a length of glossy tights.

Many years later I realised that perhaps one reason for Mum appearing to mellow a little around this time was a milestone in her and Dad's personal life. In April 1970 my parents had finally been able to marry and a photograph I discovered after my mother's death shows them both radiating happiness on the steps of my Grandma's house; at last the story that I told in *From Pillar to Post* had come full circle.

Mum and Dad, 1970.

We started looking for our own house and decided on Bath. We already knew the city and it was approximately half way between our parents' homes. One Saturday morning we strapped Dylan into his plastic car-seat and set off in the Cheltenham direction where we would pick up the A46 and then drive down the southerly ridge of the Cotswolds to Bath. As we dropped down from the high ground towards the junction with the A4 we formed our plan for the day.

'I seem to remember most of the estate agents are pretty close to one another, but we'll buy a Bath Chronicle first and then we won't miss any,' said Bryn. 'We'll try to get into a long-stay car-park.'

'I'm still not sure what sort of house we'll be able to buy,' I contemplated. 'We've saved £600 for our deposit so with twenty per cent needed for an older house we should be able to afford £3,000, but what will it buy us?'

'We are set on something older aren't we?' Bryn checked. 'Something with a bit of character? I've grown to like old places now.'

'Definitely,' I agreed as I parked the car and stretched in the boot for Dylan's pushchair.

Two hours later we were ready for a cup of tea and beans on toast so we crammed into a tiny café and I sat Dylan on my lap while Bryn spread out the pile of estate agents' details on the formica-topped table.

'We need to get a feel for all these districts,' I sighed. 'Let's put the sheets into some sort of order then look at that map they gave us.'

The names meant nothing to us; we hadn't strayed much beyond the city centre when we rented a flat here three years ago. Finally we had some sort of running order and made our way back to the car with the names ringing in our ears: Odd Down, Twerton and Newbridge. We soon discovered that many of these areas were so far from the city centre we may as well live in Bristol. They had little of the flavour of the Georgian terraces we hoped for and soon we felt despondent.

'I've made notes on the details as we've seen the houses,' reported Bryn. 'I suppose some of them might be OK and have something to recommend them to make up for their location.'

'Like price?' I queried sarcastically. 'Let's go home now. Dylan has been so good and it's not going to last. We're all tired now. Tomorrow we can think about what to do next.'

Dylan was a delightful child; he had a sunny personality that matched his golden hair. He was ready for anything and seemed to enjoy the constant changes of scenery we provided for him. He was strong and sturdy and took an interest in everything around him joining in with a ready smile and a few words. His vocabulary had developed quickly – we were always talking to him or singing and he was able to ask for things in two-word sentences. He was the apple of our eyes and Bryn loved buying him new toys that developed his dexterity and reactions. He behaved so well when we took him out that I didn't want to take advantage of his amenable nature.

Over the next few weekends we made a few more journeys south to look at houses. By then we had received sheaves of details from the estate agents we'd registered with. A good third of them we chucked in the bin straight away because we thought them ugly houses, another third we dismissed because of location and the rest were on our list of possible viewings but we needed more properties in our price range; we hadn't really seen anything that matched up to our dreams. I wanted a house with a garden that I could make something of: I always felt disappointed when I went into the garden of our rented house. The yard of blue-bricks passed a tiny flower bed where I stuck a few plants cadged from Mum and then it led on to a concrete path straight down the middle of a ragged patch of grass that counted as a lawn. We tried to tame it with the mower but it never looked much and in any case was surrounded by rusting corrugated-iron fences bulging off their rotten posts. I came from a family of keen gardeners and felt I would like to put my stamp on a patch of my own. Bryn had lived all his life in a flat where the washing line swung over a steep path trodden through tall grass sheltering wild cyclamen and violets and sometimes a chair was dragged outside the back door to catch the late sun; he didn't seem to mind not having a garden.

In July, just after my twenty-sixth birthday we were ready to move; we had finally made our choice. We had viewed properties nearer and nearer the town centre and had been getting fed up with spending weekend after weekend trying to make a short-list of three or four houses.

'This is much harder than I thought,' I had grizzled. 'We've looked at the poet avenues off Bear Flat, the houses round the Triangle at Oldfield Park and dismissed the ones too near the Bristol Road.'

'Let's take another look at that map. Chuck it over!' Bryn sighed. 'The way I see it we're going in ever decreasing circles like rabbits in the headlights but at least it concentrates the area. It looks like we've subconsciously decided that our southern boundary is the railway line and our western one is Victoria Park;

the houses to the east of London road are all big and turned into flats so surely we've defined the only places left,' he had said organizationally in a rare logical flash, for it was I who usually made the decisions.

We had sorted and sifted the diminishing pile of estate agents details and decided to review our options. We had to find somewhere in the tangle of streets behind the Royal Crescent and the Circus or off the London Road where the houses rose steeply in the northern reaches of Walcot parish.

'Let's do it now: let's make our short-list. We can't keep spending our precious weekends wearing out the A46! We've driven past the houses and looked at several of them; let's whittle it down to three or four,' I suggested, eager to end the state of flux we felt ourselves in.

Fifteen minutes later we had them: one off Julian Road, one in Highbury Place, another at Perfect View and the last house at Claremont.

We noticed that in many districts of the city there were boarded-up houses that spoke of disuse and neglect; perfectly good houses too. Some had broken windows and the drain-pipes were coming adrift from others. Some of them looked as though demolition would be the next step and these shabby terraces gave the area a seedy, down-at-heel look. The area around Julian Street was such a place and we decided to cross it off our list.

The remaining three houses were very close to each other and we made our final selection after an extended viewing appointment. The next step was the Cheltenham and Gloucester Building Society where we had been saving our money for six years and we felt sure there would be no problem securing an eighty percent mortgage of £2,500 on the delightful house that we had chosen.

Chapter 4

🌿 Highbury Place, Bath 🌿

This then, was the house of my dreams; an austere, flat-fronted late Regency house with a solid six-panelled front door beside a classic sash window. This was the house for which we had foregone foreign holidays, new cars and smart new furniture. The first-floor window had a tiny iron balcony that confirmed its period and the top floor windows were on a slightly smaller scale. It was in a terrace of ten houses situated high on the hillside above the modern Snowhill development off the London Road and commanded fabulous views across the city towards Claverton Down with Sham Castle on the high horizon. The terrace rose gently up the gradient of Highbury Place and then the road surface became loose rubble as it passed more period properties.

The especial beauty of the site was that no houses had been built opposite; the view was open. I found it hard to believe; our garden lay on the other side of the road, sprawling down a south-easterly slope. There was a pear tree, a lawn and some weedy flower borders but the garden held the promise of a delightful haven.

We had far more belongings now than when we had moved in 1967; for one thing we had managed to enlarge our stock of furniture with pieces cadged, rescued or bought cheaply; for another thing we had all the paraphernalia that went with a child. The furniture lorry that had carted our belongings down from Evesham lumbered up the approach, locked into reverse and negotiated the bad bend at the bottom of our road to draw up outside the house where we were waiting with the keys in our hand.

My parents were looking after Dylan for a couple of days and would bring him down to us when Dad was scheduled to come to check over the electrics. We had two days to get a feel for our new abode and put our belongings into some sort of order. Once everything was unloaded and the van had departed we gave each other nervous glances and walked slowly round the house wondering what we had let ourselves in for. We had only seen it twice before and our main point of reference had been the building society's valuation and survey sheet.

Forty eight hours later and Dad's Mini ground up the hill to Highbury Place. Mum unwrapped herself elegantly from the cramped car, liberated Dylan from the harness of his child-seat and rang the ornate bell as Dad lifted cable, electrical fittings, tool box and his Black and Decker drill from the small boot.

Mum did the honours with the sherry bottle produced from her holdall as we cuddled Dylan and listened to his chatter. Inevitably my parents wanted to look round our new house as soon as possible and Dad wanted to see what he had let himself in for in the way of upgrading the electrics.

Bryn reached for the surveyors report in its by now dog-eared envelope.

'Luckily they didn't retain any of the mortgage money but there are a few conditions attached,' he began tentatively.

'I knew it wouldn't be straightforward,' my mother interjected. 'Why you had to buy such an old house I don't know. It's going to need a lot of work,' sniping I knew at Bryn's lack of expertise in practical do-it-yourself skills.

'Come on then; let's do the tour,' Dad suggested, deflecting a contentious subject. 'Where shall we start?'

We all trooped out into the stone flagged hall and made for the half-glazed door leading into the courtyard at the back.

'That's lovely!' Mum exclaimed as we entered a rather dilapidated conservatory.

'Yes, we thought so too,' I agreed, 'but you see that cast iron post there? Well, look up. It supports the corner of that structure poking out from the back of the house one floor up. That is the toilet and the surveyor didn't like it. He says we've got to knock all this down and put the loo in the bathroom, so we won't have a conservatory.'

'Never mind, dear, if you whitewash all these walls it could look quite attractive with pot plants – something bright like geraniums. Shame the houses in the road above you look right down into this space,' she couldn't help adding.

'Let's go to the dining room next,' I suggested, turning the group in the hall and passing into the room at the back of the house.

I liked this room; it had real atmosphere with its huge built-in pine dresser stretching right across the wall and lit by the adjacent window. Opposite the dresser was a fireplace with a cast-iron grate with hobs each side where I'd rested Gran's copper kettle.

'Well this is more like it,' exclaimed Mum. 'I can begin to see the appeal now. There isn't much wrong in here is there?'

'Well it's a bit damp at the back of the cupboards and under the window,' Bryn offered.' The thing is there's a lack of electric sockets and we wondered if Dad could add a couple.'

'Should be possible,' Dad assured us. 'Is the kitchen through there?' he asked peering over my shoulder. 'I suspect that will need a bit of up-dating.'

We passed into the long kitchen and I noticed their noses twitch at the smell of damp.

'We've got to have a damp course put in too,' I told them before they asked. 'We'll show you upstairs now.'

We moved one by one up the stone staircase to the half landing.

'That's the toilet that juts out at the back,' Bryn said, nodding at the door. 'And this is the bathroom where they want us to put it,' he added passing along the landing up a few more steps. He proudly opened the door with a flourish revealing a huge room with a fireplace and ceiling-high cupboards in the alcoves.

'Phew! That will be a chilly place to have a bath,' Mum commented icily.

'There's a lot of work that will have to be done here,' Bryn sighed. 'We'll have to put in a new bathroom suite and hot water system. The geyser's had it and I would feel safer with an immersion heater.'

'You're telling me!' Dad said. 'I can run the cables in for you if it will help.'

I knew the main bedroom would surprise them with its sheer size and ushered them through the door without an introduction. Dad made for the large window and took in the superb view while Mum just stood in the doorway casting her eyes round the cavernous room, over twice the size of their bedroom in Redditch.

'Well my dears, it's lovely but it will take a few tins of paint,' was her only comment.

'We can't make up our mind whether this will be our bedroom or whether we will be on the top floor next to Dylan's room,' I supplied. 'It's quite a temptation to be here as it's got much higher ceilings but the room above is just as big.' I led the five of us up the next flight; wooden stairs this time.

The two rooms mirrored the size of the accommodation below but didn't feel so airy; the windows were smaller too.

'This will be your room,' we showed Dylan. 'What a lot of space you'll have!' I thought of his single bed, chair and big pine chest of drawers and wondered what else would fill the room. It would be too cold to be a play-room and in any case we wouldn't want to isolate Dylan up here on his own.

'Well, what do you think?' I asked my parents. 'Great isn't it?' I enthused without waiting for an answer. 'A real slice of history! Whoever thought we would own a regency house in Bath?'

Dad stood on the top landing and looked up to the sky-light high above where you could glimpse the angles of the roof coming down to a hidden centre-valley.

'Yes, that's on the list too. It leaks very slightly,' I grimaced. 'But you can get up there and sit down! It's fantastic!' I could only see the positive in our exciting new venture.

After Mum and I had made up a bed on the old studio-couch we told them the whole story. The Cheltenham and Gloucester insisted that we should complete the work within six months; that was a condition of the mortgage. We needed to start getting estimates as soon as possible so we could find out how much we were going to have to stump up. We could get a renovation grant for fifty per cent of the cost but it would mean we had to do all the work at once, not as and when we could afford it. Needless to say, we had put all our savings up-front for our deposit and worse than that we were one pay-packet down.

'I suppose I could get a small part-time job' I mused, 'but it would have to be in the evenings once Bryn has come home from work to look after Dylan.'

'Hard work never hurt anybody,' Mum declared. 'I've slogged my guts out for you kids.'

I knew that as soon as my parents had returned home we would have to get some builders in and I would have to start searching the situations vacant columns if we were going to enjoy living in our dream house. A couple of days later as we stood in front of the pale blue front door to wave them goodbye with the stone façade of our house glowing in the light reflected back from the golden city we were hit by the full impact of what we had taken on.

I soon found a suitable job: a part-time youth leader was needed at a club at Larkhall and my involvement with the church youth club and Young Farmers and my experience as a Sunday school teacher seemed to convince them that I had something to offer. I worked two evenings a week and soon realised that I was out of my depth. Things had moved on a bit since I had told bible stories and sung hymns. Even my experiences at Young Farmers Club were out-moded. These young people bored easily with darts and table tennis; all they seemed to need was loud pop music, endless cups of coffee and plenty of the opposite sex. Girls crowded round me to tell me about their boyfriends and to surprise me with their exploits. They asked my advice about when it was safe to have sex, about how far to go with petting and if I knew where contraception was available. I felt like an agony aunt in a teenage magazine and was desperately inadequate in my role of advisor.

My pay was essential to keep us solvent and we hadn't even started to put any money on one side for our renovation budget. I knew I would have to keep this job.

The estimates had come in from three builders and we had submitted them together with our grant application form to the council. We would have to find two-hundred pounds as our share and we remembered how long it had taken to accumulate our deposit money. It was hanging over us like a cloud. Neither set of parents had any savings so we couldn't borrow from them; they all struggled to pay the rent on their own homes. We couldn't borrow money, full stop. There was no way we could pay interest on a loan.

Bryn started to get depressed about it saying we should have stayed in rented accommodation. I was sure something would work out; surely we wouldn't be evicted from our own house just because we couldn't complete the work within the six-month deadline. I loved this house and I wouldn't let it go without a struggle. I suggested that we start some of the cosmetic work on the property. Surely if we put our own stamp on it with our personal style of decorating we would feel more secure.

We began up on the top floor in our huge bedroom. In the heat of high summer with the windows flung open we started to peel off the wads of encrusted wallpaper. Layer upon layer had been added to the walls and the scraps showed the history of the house through the decades. Finally we saw the brown flecked walls as we levered off the thick chunks with the wide scrapers. Suddenly we both realised that the other one had started to scratch their arms, and then their chest and neck. In seconds we were aware of insects jumping off the walls onto our exposed skin and I shrieked.

'Crikey! I think they are fleas! Squash the blighters!'

Our panic upset Dylan playing placidly in his playpen on the far side of the room.

'Let's get out of here,' Bryn shouted, frantically brushing his arms as he dashed towards Dylan. 'Just shut the door and make a run for it.'

The next morning after Bryn had left for work I counted about sixty bites on my body. I went down to the phone box and contacted the council. Yes, they assured me, someone from Pest Control would be round as soon as possible. I thought ahead, feeling embarrassed: would the neighbours be able to identify the van? Would they think we kept a mucky house? Would they make judgements about us before we had even got to know them?

At ten o'clock a plain white van arrived and the boiler-suited men walked all round the house surveying the rooms and all the nooks and crannies.

'It seems like the fleas have been lying dormant under the wallpaper,' one man explained. 'They live on the starch in the old fashioned flour paste. As long as it wasn't disturbed you were alright.'

I shuddered in disbelief wondering how they were going to deal with it.

'We'll have to spray the whole house. You must leave all the drawers and cupboards open in all the rooms so the fumes can get in and we'll mist all the walls down with an insecticide. Can you sleep somewhere else?'

I explained our situation and we decided the best they could do would be to carry out the work immediately while Dylan and I took ourselves out for the day. Then I would call and tell Bryn at work and we would delay our return until as late as possible. I didn't much fancy sleeping in a house reeking of insecticide but there was no other option. At six-thirty we unlocked the door and were relieved to note that it wasn't too bad. We had instructions to leave everything exposed over-night, then in the morning I could restore order. Once we had finished stripping the walls I could repaper them on my own while Bryn was at work and I soon had all the imperfections covered up with coarse textured wood-chip paper, ready to paint primrose yellow. We followed this room with Dylan's and moved on to paint the sitting room.

We were feeling more settled now and had started to put five-pounds a week on one side as our renovation budget. Over the months that cash would provide one hundred pounds towards our total leaving us miserably short of our target. In early September we saw an advertisement in the Bath Chronicle asking for accommodation for university students. We discussed the possibility of sharing our house and put the pros and cons to each other.

'The only room someone could use is the big front room on the first-floor,' I confirmed. 'It's big enough for a bed, a table and some easy chairs.'

'Yes, but it's the best room in the house,' countered Bryn. 'I thought we might use it some day.'

'But this won't be for ever. It's an emergency measure to increase our savings,' I argued. 'Either we want to stay here or we don't. We've got to try anything to keep the house.'

'I don't think I'll like it if anyone else is living here. They wouldn't be able to eat with us.' I could tell that Bryn was not as committed as I to saving the house.

'We've got to suffer a little bit. Nothing is ever straight forward,' I reminded him. 'Perhaps they can buy their meals at the university refectory. Young people don't eat breakfast these days. They could have a kettle to make drinks. I suggest we ring the accommodation officer and talk it over.'

Two days later a capable woman with a clip-board arrived to look at the room we had on offer and to check the bathroom facilities. She agreed the room could be let on a 'no-meals' basis and told us we could ask for three guineas a week in rent. We took twenty-four hours to make up our minds and then asked to be placed on the register of inspected lodgings. They would send three prospective student-tenants round the week before term started in early October.

Meanwhile we bought a brass bedstead from a second hand stall and stood it against the dramatic bottle-green painted back wall. There was a bedside cabinet with a lamp and an old chest of drawers to complete the bedroom section. We put an easy chair each side of the fireplace with another lamp on the low alcove cupboards. Over towards the window stood a sanded and green-painted dining table complemented by two chairs; this would serve as a study area. Lucky student, we thought. It all looked serene and delightful, a perfect place to work and live and what with the magnificent view we felt that the room we offered would be snapped up by the first-comer.

We had begun to make friends and contacts in the city. We picked up our friendship with Stephen and Pat Beck who lived up at Claverton Down. We had met them through the British Model Society when Bryn was an active member and when the men's talk was of warfare and uniforms I talked to Pat about children and Dylan's development.

Bryn knew people at the Film Society but I felt rather left out as I had to stay at home now to look after Dylan. We went long walks together with Dylan in his strong Restmore pushchair and often ended up in the delightful Victoria Park. Some days I would walk into town and meet Bryn for lunch and we would share sandwiches sitting on a bench near St James Parade where Bryn worked for the Blackett Press and Dylan would sit tucked up under his yellow plaid blanket munching an apple slice.

We had got to know another family in Highbury Place; they lived a little further up the hill at number ten. Their house was undergoing renovation also; I had glanced inside the open front door as I pushed Dylan past. The floor-boards were up from the front door to the back and the walls were stripped back to bare plaster – we had that in common. The next time I walked up the road I got into conversation with a bohemian looking woman and she invited us inside. Her children were a little older and were playing with some blocks of wood on the dusty floor. I established an immediate rapport with Heather and leant back comfortably on the battered sofa covered with an old shawl. They were both involved in artistic projects and examples of their work dotted the room. Over the next few weeks we would meet at each other's house or in the garden if it was sunny and Dylan began to learn how to socialise with other children.

Mid-summers Day came and went and as the weather got hotter and more sultry storm clouds would gather over the city. The huge, grey cumulo-stratus clouds would roll along the top of Claverton Down opposite and suddenly a fork of lightening might leap across the sky from hill to hill. A deluge would shroud the city from view and I would feel like one of the gods conducting the electric storm as the thunder crashed from the percussion section. The elemental excitement was tremendous as I watched flash after flash of lightening and as the rain lashed against the windows the hairs stood up on the back of my neck.

As summer turned to autumn the trees across the valley took on the colours or amber and ochre, of russet and terracotta. I loved this house as I had not loved our previous three homes and looked forward to the tenant whose rent would save the house for us.

The first student to look at the accommodation was Ashok from Iran and he took no persuading that it would suit him. He agreed the rent set by the university accommodation officer and asked when he could bring his belongings round. He settled in quickly but things did not go well for very long. He liked to lie late in bed and often skipped his lectures. I couldn't keep to my cleaning schedule for his room and neither could I change the bed-linen. Once I did manage to find a slot when he wasn't in occupation I had twice the work to do. The bed hadn't been made for weeks and clothes littered every surface, the room was very untidy and the bin over-flowed with empty whisky bottles. This was not what I had in mind when we had decided to let a room. I had to shrug off my feelings of discontent and concentrate on the fact that the rent would put us nearer our target of two hundred pounds.

Worse was to come; one day I returned to the house to hear the noise of running water coming from the dining room. I was horrified to see water streaming down the back wall where the built-in dresser was. We stored many of our over-sized books on these wide pine shelves as well as pieces of Granny's china and our attempts at sketching. I raced up stairs to the bathroom: the taps were running and the geyser was going full tilt, the room was full of steam and condensation ran down the walls – Ashok was nowhere to be seen. I turned the taps off and hammered on his door. A sleepy reply came and he emerged in his underwear. He had run the bath and gone back to bed and then drifted off to sleep. I was furious and marched him downstairs to show him the damage and flung a few choice words at him. I spent the next hour wiping down the books and spreading the pages out to minimize the damage but knew that the buckled covers and corrugated pages would remain for ever. That evening when recounting the tale to Bryn we decided to increase our lodger's rent from three guineas (three pounds, three shillings) a week to four pounds to compensate for the damage.

The final straw came only a week later when I went in our lodger's bedroom to vacuum the floor. The electric fire had been left on and it was facing a damp towel draped over the bed presumably to dry it out. That evening we told him that the end of term would be the end of his lease; we couldn't afford to put the safety of our house at risk. When we told the accommodation officer she said she suspected that our tenant had been used to having maids to do the menial jobs at home.

The garden had turned into a matted tangle of dying plants as November passed into December and any spare time I had I would cross the road to our patch to restore order. Just below the hard standing for a car was the lawn which looked smarter now it had benefited from four months trimming with our Qualcast mower and the flower-beds I had rejuvenated just needed the dead heads of golden rod, lupins and aquilegia cutting back to ground level. The lavender bushes were already trim from the shearing I had given them when I harvested the flower heads to dry. Further down the slope rose-bay willow herb and buddleia had taken over but I had plans for next year and looked forward to establishing a vegetable patch.

Christmas was looming up and I began to make some presents to give to family members. I fashioned book-marks and made lavender bags, then mounted a few of my sketches in frames bought from the stall in the market. Bryn and I spent a weekend designing and printing our Christmas cards from lino-cuts and then made a few decorations for our Christmas tree.

Dylan and Angie, Malvern early 1971.

I pondered over what I could make for our new friends up the hill, Steve, Heather and family. Finally I decided to cover the top of a wooden box with foam and upholster it as a stool. I tacked braid round the edge and the domed brass pins gave it a seasonal gleam. A few days before Christmas I took the gift up to the house and handed it over with the season's greetings and Heather moved over to an old trunk and reached inside for two presents wrapped in tissue paper. On Christmas morning we discovered a furry dark brown bear for Dylan and a stick of firewood carved into a woman in a long skirt for us. Having these hand-made presents given with affection made us realise how lucky we were to have found these unconventional friends.

January 1971 meant that our deadline for completing our building work was only a matter of weeks away and we hadn't even got the money together yet. During the short grey days of the new year we argued about what to do.

'I can't see how we can stay here,' groaned Bryn.

'You don't think the Building Society will actually bother to send someone out to inspect such a trivial job, do you? I responded.

'Yes, they might just,' said Bryn pessimistically. 'Even if we had the money now the work couldn't start for weeks.'

'Surely that's to our advantage? We can say we want to hold off until the better weather and that will stall them,' I was thinking of any and every way we could get through the next few months until we had enough cash saved to employ a builder.

'Even if we managed to get the work done this spring there will be more expense. I never seem to have a penny for myself!' Bryn retorted. 'I work as many hours as I can and there's hardly anything left over for even a newspaper. I'm getting fed up with it.'

'But we knew that when we moved here. We knew we would have to make sacrifices. It won't be for ever, I'll try and get a better job,' I concluded, trying to pour oil on troubled waters.

I had noticed Bryn getting more dispirited as the months went by. He didn't have the same enthusiasm for this house as I did. I looked on it as a long-term plan, a project that would take years but be so worth while when we had a comfortable, stylish, classic home of our own. Bryn was more concerned with the cost of a cinema ticket or a magazine and looked towards short-term gratification.

He still corresponded about politics, jazz and model soldiers with people from all over the world so I was never surprised to see him hunched over his note pad covering it with his wild, scrawling writing.

One of the letters he wrote must have been to a former colleague at the Journal Press in Evesham because one day he read out a portion of a reply that said word had got back to the works' manager at the printing factory and he had hinted that he would be prepared to take Bryn back onto the payroll, all he would need was a letter.

We spent evening after evening talking through our options and Bryn said he thought we had over-stepped ourselves by buying this house. He knew that we could easily move back into rented accommodation in Evesham so that is what he recommended us doing. Finally I gave in and decided we may as well cut our losses and put 6, Highbury Place on the market just five and a half months after we had moved in.

A few weeks later the house was sold for two hundred and fifty pounds more than we had paid for it – just enough money to cover our legal fees. Our savings would go towards estate agent's costs and the removal lorry. As we packed our belongings into the tea-chests I felt that our relationship had dimmed a little, I sensed that Bryn had failed to find that inner strength and determination that was needed and was reluctant to reduce our already low standard of living merely for a house.

I decided to try and put this episode behind us and move on, although in truth I would never forget what we nearly had.

Chapter 5

🍃 Back to Kings Road, Evesham 🍃

It was with mixed feelings on a bleak afternoon early in 1971 that I turned left at Bengeworth roundabout, Evesham, and drove the three of us down Kings Road, a road we knew well for we had already lived there for two-and-a-half years.

Our new home was on the same side of the road as our previous house just a dozen or so doors further down. Once again it belonged to the printing firm and we drew up outside the house feeling a sense of déjà vu for we had passed it so many times on our way to the corner shop just two doors away. We had time to unlock the door and go in to open up the windows before the furniture lorry arrived and we walked round inspecting our latest home.

The house was in the typical red brick of the district and the left one of a group of three; an engraved tablet set high on the frontage proclaimed the group as Clinton Villas built in 1905. The recessed porch stood smartly at the end of a short path of chequered quarry tiles and a semi-circular arch of smoothly cut stone dominated the opening topped by a wedge-shaped keystone. The entrance hall was lit by the pale wintry sun filtering through the frosted glass of the half-glazed front door.

The internal layout was different to our other house up the road. Here the lounge was to the left and seemed smaller without the bay window. There was a tiled fireplace with a few ashes in the grate and we guessed it had been occupied until fairly recently.

The staircase went across the house between the two main rooms and the short hall ended abruptly with a door to the living room. We were pleased to see that this was a large room, the full width of the house and would take both the dining table and easy chairs and the fireplace was flanked by alcoves in the traditional style. A sash window showed us a view of the back garden which ended with the side wall of a dilapidated, bitumen-coated garage. We passed through a door directly into the kitchen which was not as old-fashioned as we had dreaded. At least it was easily accessible from the living room and hopefully would not be too cold once we had the paraffin stove secured to the wall and lit. We decided it was time to buy our first fridge to slot under a work top for this house didn't have a pantry.

We made our way up the stairs which ended outside the door of the main bedroom. Once again we were impressed; this front room was full width, stretching above both lounge and hallway and we mentally fitted in our bulky bedroom furniture.

Dylan's bedroom overlooked the back garden and was a good size. We began to realise that this house had potential. As usual the bathroom was isolated at the rear of the house above the kitchen but we were used to cold bathrooms – we had never known any different – and another oil-stove would help to take the edge off the chill.

This was it then: our home, for now at least. The rent was two pounds a week and I had seen the relief in Bryn's face when we had done our sums before moving. The house would be maintained by the landlord, his employer, but we were free to decorate it as we wished and best of all there would be no mortgage to pay and no builder's bills to meet.

I was not so convinced about the merits of our move back to Evesham. Yes, granted we had shelved the problems that had loomed in Bath; the deadline imposed by the Cheltenham and Gloucester Building Society, the anxiety of having to come up with the cash for the building work, and the realisation that we had chosen a house that would never be free from tricky ongoing maintenance but hadn't we just moved back to the things we were trying to escape? Bryn had long been wanting to get employment in another company in the hope of improved conditions and in any case hadn't he said he was keen to move from Evesham with its flat uneventful landscape of cabbage fields and orchards? Hadn't he railed against the parochial attitudes of his workmates, condemning them for not standing up to be counted when it came to voting in Union meetings? Had he not despaired at the lack of arts facilities and venues? Furthermore this house was once again tied to Bryn's job and he hated the feeling that our security could be compromised by his need to speak out. What were we doing back here? The answer was that he had persuaded me that we needed an easy life, one that was mapped out with a regular pay-packet and enough surplus money to buy the odd record or magazine and a few new clothes once he had fulfilled his responsibilities to the household account and Dylan's needs. It seemed to me that for Bryn the grass was always greener on the other side of the fence.

Here we were then, and I thought I may as well make the best of it. Getting the house sorted out would be a challenge I would enjoy although I was already thinking about the unwanted influence of Mum. Whilst living at Highbury Place I had come to a realization that there was another way of doing things. Previously I had believed that the ultimate aim was to have a home that was spotlessly pristine in every aspect, furniture, floor covering, decoration, and that everything must be tidy and well ordered. Now I realised that a fitted carpet wasn't the be-all and end-all to a happy existence any more than the idea that everything must be colour co-ordinated. I wanted a looser, more informal style and rather than spending days on housework I would prefer to play with our child or take him for walks. Would it be too late I wondered, after five years of married life to make such an about turn, especially in the face of likely disapproval from Mum?

As with all our previous four moves we couldn't afford for Bryn to have time off work to sort things out; in any case he would not be due any holidays until he had worked there for a few months. It was down to me to get things unpacked and put away on Monday; all we needed to do that first weekend was lug the furniture into place and sort out the beds and the kitchen.

We all settled in much better than I thought we would. Dylan's easy going personality meant that it seemed like a big adventure to him and once he was surrounded by all his favourite toys – his teddy and bunny rabbit and his trike and building blocks – he adapted easily to his new home.

Surprisingly, Bryn seemed happy at work too. The Journal Press had a new contract, the printing of a prestigious antique and collector's magazine; the standard of the colour printing was high and once again Bryn was able to take a pride in his craft. A bonus of this was that proof copies taken from the first few pulls through the press and then glued-up in the binding room were often discarded. Each month Bryn managed to secure a spare copy for Mum and Dad.

They had continued to build up their beautiful home and often browsed round antique shops hoping to find a bargain that just needed a touch of tender loving care. The magazine helped them to recognise periods and quality and they pored over the various articles as each monthly edition was given pride of place on the coffee table in their sitting room.

Dylan, 95 Kings Road, June 1972.

I had reached a truce with my mother and we seemed to be getting on better. She and Dad loved looking after Dylan for us and this gave us the freedom to go shopping in Birmingham once we had dropped him off at Redditch on the way. They warmed to his pliant and affectionate ways and led him round the beautiful garden at South Street showing him the pretty goldfish pond and the bird bath and the wind blowing in the huge balsam poplar tree. Sometimes they would take him a drive in the Mini down to the water-splash to fish for minnows or sometimes down to the chip shop in Grove Street for a packet of fish and chips.

Dylan loved books and absorbed all the stories we could read him. As he approached his second birthday we completed an application form for his first junior library ticket and then each week I would take him in his pushchair up through the town to the Library in the Market Place to get two or three more picture books. Each evening before bedtime Bryn would take Dylan on his lap and follow the words on the page with his finger then point to the illustrations in the attractive books.

At Easter we went down to Torquay for our visit to Bryn's Mum. Dylan loved his visit to Paignton Zoo with his Granny and was excited by his trip to Goodrington sands one blustery afternoon.

At home I worked hard on our garden all spring and was rewarded by shows of delphiniums and lupins, tall white daisies and pink roses. The crowning glory of the garden was a wooden, working windmill that Dad had made for his grandson's second birthday. It dwarfed Dylan who was delighted when the red-tipped sails turned in the breeze against the white painted mill.

Our family was coming together and we felt contented and settled. We decided to try for another child and I soon became pregnant. Our happiness was short lived as once again I went through the trauma of a miscarriage and had to be hospitalized in Worcester. After relying on Dad and Mum to take him there at visiting times which meant a very long round trip for them Bryn decided it was time to learn to drive.

Once I was back home and passed as fit we consoled ourselves with a holiday in Cornwall. Our last trip to Cornwall when Dylan was only a few months old had ended prematurely when a plague of flies had compromised hygiene arrangements in our holiday cottage. This time with our son as a sturdy two-year-old we were able to explore more of this fascinating county and ventured down Rocky Valley near Tintagel, drove up onto the high moors to Chun Quoit and down the estuary past Falmouth to see Pendennis Castle perched on the headland to the south of the river. As ever our guide books were Daphne du Maurier's *Vanishing Cornwall* and John Betjeman's *Shell Guide to Cornwall.*

I decided to look for a part-time job to give us some extra cash to buy things for the house. It would have to be in the evenings of course, once Bryn had come home from work and was free to look after Dylan and put him to bed. I applied for a cleaning job at Avonside hospital and went for an interview. That evening I told Bryn all about it.

'The hours are from six until nine in the evening,' I said hopefully. 'Five evenings a week, of course. Still, I won't have to do weekends.'

'That doesn't give me much time, does it,' Bryn answered. 'By the time I've cycled home, washed and changed it will be half past five.'

'That's OK isn't it? You'll have had your main meal at lunch time so I'll just need to make you a plate of sandwiches and cut a slice of cake and then you can take over looking after Dylan.' I countered.

'I'll have to put him to bed and everything,' Bryn said with a nervous edge to his voice.

'Look: I'll wash him and put him ready in his pyjamas and I can leave him strapped in his chair while you have tea. You enjoy reading him his story.' I replied. 'You'll just have to put him on the potty and tuck him up in bed.'

'Well I suppose so,' he reluctantly agreed. 'But it will be a bit miserable for me, all on my own.'

'Do we need the money or not!' I retorted rhetorically. 'I wouldn't mind some new clothes, Dyl is growing out of his and we keep seeing things we'd like for the house. We can't survive for ever on cast-offs!' I didn't give him a chance to butt in, 'Do you think it will be a picnic for me, going out to work for three hours when I've spent the day looking after a two-year-old, doing housework, shopping and laundry and also acting as gardener and house decorator?'

'No, you're right. The money will be very useful,' Bryn agreed calmly, trying to placate me. 'What else did they say at the interview?'

'Well, I was able to choose between cleaning the wards as a member of a team or tackling the long, two storey office block on my own. I chose the offices – I thought I would prefer to take sole responsibility for my work. I hope I've made the right decision.'

'When will you know?' Bryn asked.

'In a few days, although I think it's just a matter of checking references,' I concluded.

I received the answer I wanted and started work the following week in September, just as the nights were drawing in. My work involved emptying bins, cleaning toilets, washing up mugs then dusting the paper-littered desks and filing cabinets and finally dragging the vacuum cleaner the length of the building on two floors. It was tiring work but I knew if we wanted things we saw in the shops I'd have to stick at it. We still worked on our original arrangement of splitting surplus money 50:50 between us whether it was ten shillings or five pounds so I agreed to do that with my earnings.

That Christmas we invited Bryn's Mum up to Evesham to stay with us. Sadly her husband had died in Exvale hospital after increasing symptoms of premature senility and in many ways I think she was relived that the burden of care had been lifted. It must have been heart-breaking to see someone you love and had lived with for well over thirty years fade gently into an unknown and unknowing world. Needless to say we met up with my family and passed a very sociable time over the festive season.

* * * * *

Bryn and I started 1972 feeling confident and united; everything seemed to be going better for us. We had bought some new *avant garde* furniture for our house – a black plastic inflatable chair and a blue canvas butterfly chair where the fabric stretched over a spindly metal frame like wings. These took pride of place in our newly decorated lounge where we had a contemporary wallpaper and plain carpet.

I was making new friends in the district, there was Margaret and Aggie, Christine and Molly and I met them all in turn while our children played together. I drove over to Honeybourne to visit a friend I'd made in the maternity hospital and her son Christopher would share his toys with Dylan for an afternoon. Dave Woods, my old friend from childhood, had married and I was godmother to his first child, Cheryl. Each week I would rush through my chores, load Dylan into his car seat and drive over to spend the day with Wendy and Cheryl at South Littleton.

Since marriage I had slightly drifted apart from my old friend Sylvia. We had shared all our secrets since the age of eight but we saw each other infrequently now. I still loved to receive her news and was delighted when she became a State Registered Nurse from the Queen Elizabeth Hospital, Birmingham. She was making plans to nurse at the protestant hospital in the Ivory Coast and moved there in July.

We had super neighbours too: Mr & Mrs Dawson, a nice elderly couple on one side and Mr Stanton in a semi-detached on the other side. I often took Dylan round for a cup of tea with Mr Stanton. He confined his use of his big house to the back living room and kitchen and lived quite a lonely existence. Before his retirement he was a baker and he still enjoyed turning out a batch of cakes and took a pride in offering them round. I loved to hear his tales of old Evesham and once he had got going on a story he was almost unstoppable. Sometimes he would offer to take Dylan and me out for a drive in his huge Morris Oxford car and he would wedge his not insubstantial bulk behind the wheel and we would set off at a sedate pace of twenty-five miles an hour to tour the Vale of Evesham or the Cotswolds.

The other side of Mr Stanton's house lived the Fairbrothers, Elsie and Bill and their son John. Elsie and I became friends and in her shy and hesitant way she would confide in me the difficulties of being at 'a certain time of life.'

A bonus of being a housewife was that your time was your own in which to plan your chores and to work twice as hard to compact them into half a day if it gave you chance to go out. With this in mind I made regular trips to see both my aunties.

Auntie Chris had recently moved to a newly renovated flat in Malt Mill Lane, Alcester. This street of sixteenth, seventeenth and eighteenth century houses had become rather dilapidated and seedy and in 1972 Alcester Town Council had taken on the job of renovating them and returning them to use as delightful homes. On the corner of the street was the very impressive sixteenth-century Malt House with its dark oak jetties tottering out over the street. Inside was an enormous floor space where decades ago barley had been spread out to germinate and so begin the first process in beer making. The rest of Malt Mill Lane consisted of the half-timbered houses of Tudor merchants and simple red-brick cottages dating from Victorian times. The renovations began on the left hand side with the handsome house that was formerly the Excelsior Needle Factory and continued down the road the other side of a wide, oak-beamed arch which led to an ancient malt kiln.

The flat that Auntie Chris had been allocated was reached by passing under the deep arch and turning left to an entrance door in the crook of the buildings. After climbing a flight of ancient stairs the flat was entered from a wide landing. Auntie had made it charming: the well lit sitting room contained the best of Granny's furniture and an extra oak side-table made the perfect place for a stunning flower arrangement. All of my aunt's artistic skill had been put to good use with hand-embroidered cushion covers and even the home-made lampshades matched the décor. The newly installed kitchen boasted a range of units that were so different to the old table and kitchen cabinet at Granny's house that I could see the pride in Auntie's face. The flat was on two levels and as you passed from one range of historic buildings to another there was a short flight of steps. I loved the quirkiness of the apartment and could feel the history seeping through the walls. However, it would be another thirty five years before my family history research revealed that in 1881 my aunt's grandparents, James and Mary Findon, had lived in the same street with their first 4 children – her mother's brothers.

Auntie Daye's home was the other end of the spectrum. Some while ago she and her husband, Joe Greatorex, had moved into a new detached bungalow in Cladswell Lane, Cookhill. It was a well designed and spacious home with an enormous and gracious lounge decorated in a tranquil shade of lavender. The two dachshunds, Karl and Petre, had been joined by a boisterous Bassett hound much adored by Grandad while he was alive. I would try to visit Auntie Daye each week as she loved to see Dylan. If it was fine I would carry the tea tray outside where we would sit under the eponymous apple trees on the swinging sun-hammock while Dylan tottered round the neat lawn of the extensive garden. Auntie was very generous and always gave us some nice tit-bit of food to take home such as a tin of salmon or ham or anything else she could find in the larder.

Again, my later historical research showed that about two hundred yards down the lane was the thatched cottage which my ancestors had built next to the village pond when they moved there from near Droitwich at the end of the eighteenth century. This thatched house was occupied by at least five generations of Winnetts but my mother or her sisters had never mentioned it to me.

Mum and Dad seemed very happy too and this contentment was reflected in a more relaxed atmosphere when we met up – although she often sent a stinging barb in Bryn's direction aimed at reducing his rather fragile self confidence when it came to doing jobs around the house.

My parents still visited Hastings whenever they could, although the long drive was becoming a bit of an ordeal for Dad. They returned from their holiday in a mellow mood after sharing in the warm open-hearted hospitality of Dad's family where the atmosphere was relaxed and Grandma Ancell's indomitable spirit presided over the hard working household. Mum forgot all the tribulations of much earlier years and she and Auntie Stella would share a laugh when they recalled the nightmare times of the 1940's.

One day my parents received a phone call from my sister, Jean, who as a nun was now based at the convent's retreat-home at Peebles in Scotland. She had suffered from ill health for many years and had been hospitalized on several occasions; now it appeared she was ill with a severe dose of flu. The work at the retreat centre was tough and there was a shortage of nuns to perform the many tasks connected with running such a house; this meant there was no-one to nurse Jean or even fetch her a drink and she was feeling very despondent. I can only assume that she was also suffering a crisis of faith as she announced that she intended leaving the sisterhood and would bid them farewell the very next day. She had borrowed an outfit of clothes and some money from the local vicar's wife and told my parents to expect her within twenty-four hours! Mum was astounded and said she wasn't keen on having Jean living at South Street with them but Dad insisted that they must give her a home – for the time being at least. A week later I accompanied her, with her tightly cropped hair slowly growing back, to Worcester for an appointment with the Bishop to request relinquishing her Holy Vows. A few weeks later Jean had found herself a flat and a job and moved into rooms in Bromsgrove Road.

It was very pleasant to see more of my sister; despite a fourteen year age gap I had always felt close to her and thought that we shared a bond of unconventionality. When Mum made some cutting remark about her appearance or clumsiness I always sprang to Jean's defence. Jean had left

Jean on her marriage to Phil Watton.

home to work almost before I was aware of her and apart from the period when she left the first convent near Malvern and returned briefly to teaching before moving to Dorset I had not seen much of her. However, we had corresponded regularly during the years she had worked at a hardware shop in Bridport and then when she was a carer for an elderly lady. Since the mid-nineteen sixties when she entered the Sisterhood of St Peter as a novice nun at Laleham Abbey we had met only occasionally if her annual holiday happened to correspond with a family get-together. Now, I was able to help her furnish her flat and call round for tea. I was delighted when some time later she announced that she was being courted by a man from work and had developed a close affection for him.

* * * * *

In the autumn Bryn and I had some exciting news to share with the family: we were expecting another child. I had needed to have my pregnancy confirmed as early as possible because the gynaecologists had decided that I would need special treatment to avoid a third miscarriage. For thirty weeks throughout my pregnancy I had to report to Evesham Hospital for an intramuscular injection of a hormone to prevent my body from rejecting my developing baby.

'We thought it was time Dylan had a brother or sister,' I told Mum and Dad when we met up one Sunday.

'Let's hope you don't lose this one,' Mum warned.

'The doctors are going to keep a close eye on me and I've got to go to the hospital each week for special injections,' I explained.

'It's good that you are having another child; the gap was getting a bit wide,' Mum said unnecessarily as she knew we hadn't planned it like that.

'Yes, but don't forget we wanted our first child earlier and then we wanted another one two years after Dylan was born but things didn't work out,' I reminded her.

'I could see Dylan getting more and more spoilt. He needs a brother or sister to take the limelight off him,' she couldn't resist saying.

'I think we've been very fair with him. He doesn't get it all his own way,' Bryn put in, quickly.

'That's strange, coming from you – you never say 'no' to anything!' Mum bit back.

I could see our wonderful news was in danger of becoming taken over by an argument on child rearing and luckily Dad had the sense to draw it to a close by putting his arm round me and saying,

'It's wonderful news, but take it easy, ducky. Just look after yourself, alright?'

As autumn gave way to winter the lime trees along the river Avon lost their leaves and soon the cold winds started to blow across the Vale of Evesham. Redditch, which was much more exposed on its high shoulder at the northern end of The Ridgeway was even colder and stinging hail storms alternated with freezing fogs.

In the last month of the year we received some sad news: Grandma Ancell had died just after celebrating her ninetieth birthday.

Mum and Dad went down to Hastings for the funeral but Bryn and I were excused owing to me being pregnant. In the bleakest of weather with Dad suffering from his annual bout of bronchitis and joined by Uncle Peter and Auntie Elsie from Cumberland they made the journey to pay their respects to a wonderful, strong, determined and positive woman who loved fun and inspired others with her generous warm-heartedness. My parents returned home with heavy hearts and very little inclination to celebrate the forthcoming festive season and Dad seemed worn out by both the demanding drive in the Mini and his chesty cough exacerbated by the bad weather.

Not a couple to pass up a party they accepted an invitation from their old friends, Fred and Christine Nicholls. The next morning we had a visit from my brother-in-law to tell me that my father had suffered a fatal heart attack after supper and Mum had returned home after spending the night with their friends. We drove to Redditch immediately and sat holding hands with Mum in stunned silence; we were all too shocked even to weep. Christmas passed in a daze and the New Year brought the realization that I would never see my beloved father again; the father who had loved and supported me and had passed on his resourcefulness, practicality and fair-mindedness, his enquiring mind and scientific know-how. Mum was bereft and could not come to terms with the unfairness of it just as she and Dad were enjoying life with fewer worries than they had ever had and my father had planned to retire in the New Year. She could not bear to attend the internment in the cemetery when Dad was laid to rest under a tree where a robin was singing his winter song.

My pregnancy progressed with a few difficult moments and anxieties and finally on the longest day of the year our second son was born. He weighed a bonny ten pounds two ounces and had a shock of black hair. The name we had chosen for him, Luke, seemed inappropriate for such a big baby and we decided on Max which epitomised his strong constitution and already demanding personality.

I soon realised that having two children was much more difficult and seemed more like having three because there was the extra dimension of the relationship between the two siblings to contend with. Dylan did not enjoy taking second place and we did all we could to make him realise that he was loved just as much.

Right from the start Max was a vocal and boisterous baby who needed little sleep and regular feeding. As he became more active and passed from the sitting-up to the crawling stage he disrupted Dylan's quiet games with his cars and trains, knocked over his building blocks and scattered his jigsaw puzzles. At night he would not settle down to sleep and when we went to bed he was still standing up in his cot shaking it until it rattled. Dylan whose single bed was in the same room would walk in to us and tell us he couldn't sleep. Max cried and screamed for attention until the small hours and sometimes we would pick up his cot, one of us at each end, and carry it into the bathroom and shut the door on his yells so that Dylan could get to sleep.

Max began to walk at eleven months and with delight would barge into the middle of anything his brother was doing and take over the game –or destroy it.

We wondered if we were doing something wrong. Was there something we should know about sibling rivalry? Did we need to separate the brothers? Surely we didn't favour one above the other? The harder we tried to get it right the more problems we had and Dylan showed his feelings by peeing over his brother while he lay in the paddling pool the next summer.

I consulted the nurses at the Welfare Clinic and they referred me to books on child rearing and psychology. What I really needed was practical help on how to cope with the strain of children who really didn't seem to like each other. My tension led to depression and I sought advice from my doctor. Max was eighteen months old now and Dylan had been at school for two terms. Pandora's Box was opened and we were referred to family therapists, behavioural psychologists, social services and asked to keep a diary: the outcome was that Max was diagnosed as hyper-active, and they made an early play-group space available for him. His attendance went from two mornings a week, to three and eventually five mornings and this extra stimulation, both physical and mental helped to ease the situation at home. His behaviour was still unpredictable and we found the best way of dealing with potential socializing problems was to avoid the situation, which meant not going out sometimes. Supermarkets were a nightmare and any other shopping was barely tolerable. We had advice on behaviour modification and transactional analysis but the bottom line was that the specialists didn't have to cope with a screaming, rigid toddler or have to restrain him when he went berserk. I was taking anti-depressants and Max was taking juvenile tranquillisers, Bryn could barely cope at work and Dylan was falling behind at school and becoming withdrawn.

While many of our friends were rearing their children according to Dr Benjamin Spock we had decided on a rather less permissive regime for Dylan. Four years earlier we had been given a no-nonsense guide to caring for children from one to five years old. The tenet of its contents was that children should be brought up to be responsible and self-reliant and gradually, over the years, they would develop independence; in small ways at first, but then by learning the consequence of their actions so by the time they began school they were able to cope with many tasks and experiences. It had worked well for Dylan but it didn't work for Max!

Sometimes I felt weighed down with the responsibilities of parenting. I didn't feel a 'natural' at it; to me it was a skill that had to be learnt – with mixed results and I believed that just because you had decided to be a parent didn't make you automatically good at it.

When I had visualised motherhood I had seen myself as an earth-mother type and imagined doing the cleaning with a baby ledged on my hip and the duster in the other hand or patting a contentedly fed baby slung over my shoulder as I supervised a painting session at the kitchen table or made jam tarts for tea. It just wasn't like that. I was tired and irritable some times and I felt guilty that I didn't cope better.

Eventually things started to improve but we didn't seem as united in our approach as I felt we should be. We had been advised to be consistent in dealing with Max's demands and tantrums but quite often Bryn would give way to him for an easy life and I was left seeming the wicked, hard parent. It was a bad time for all of us and the dynamics of our nuclear family came under severe strain.

Mum needed us too at this time. Inevitably she was grieving for Dad and had become very introspective and bitter. She would console herself with a glass of sherry which in turn led to her becoming argumentative and critical. She and Dad had talked over the idea of him retiring soon as he had already worked on for two extra years. He had been due to finish in the New Year and they had been considering taking a new flat; one of a development of well built blocks situated in between Plymouth Road and Oakley Road on the site of the old allotments. The knowledge that they had been so close to this new stage in their life together was particularly upsetting.

* * * * *

In the middle of all this I felt that I was changing as a person. Since July 1972 and encouraged by Bryn I had been taking Spare Rib, the magazine of the Women's Liberation Movement which provided an alternative to the traditional images of women that were shown in existing magazines. Reading the latest edition each month increased my confidence and helped me to challenge sexist views and language. There was a strong belief that talking to other women was empowering and grouped together, women could bring about change in the workplace, in their environment and in their personal lives. There was little opportunity to meet with like minded women at that time and all I could do was to read more.

I took the magazine for the next ten years and as I read it each month I felt more political and dynamic. I had already joined the Campaign for Nuclear Disarmament in the early 1960's and the Anti-Blood Sports League in 1962 and as the Seventies progressed both Bryn and I had joined the Anti Nazi League, encouraged by a friend of ours who was in the Socialist Workers Party, and through the ANL tried to combat the rise of the British National Party. Now with my involvement in the Women's Movement, albeit on the periphery, I felt that I could take control of my life.

One area where I seemed to have very little control was in the employment arena. I had given up my cleaning job at Avonside Hospital, Evesham when I was about seven months pregnant and while Max was young and unmanageable I felt I couldn't go out to work, even in the evenings. I didn't like not being able to make a contribution to the household budget but I thought at least I may be able to increase my own pocket money on an occasional basis and I started making craft items to sell. A new interiors magazine called Inhabit had come out but folded after a few editions. During this time they had run a feature on knitted and crocheted cushion covers. Over several pages they had pictured about two dozen designs in a variety of geometric and abstract patterns. The colours appealed to me and I thought the intricate designs would provide a challenge to my brain which was feeling addled. I sent for the photo-copied book of patterns and went up to the wool stall in the long market hall near the Post Office to buy my first selection. I completed three cushion covers in quick succession, stuffed each with a comfy pad and gave them as presents. I loved knitting or crocheting the unusual designs and made more of them. I wanted to sell them and make some money so I approached a pine and wicker-ware shop to see if they could display them for me. Laid on the natural willow furniture they provided an unusual contrast of texture and the colours, either vibrant or muted, sang out from the honey coloured cane. They sold quickly and I made more and then received a commission for four cushions in a different colour-way, and I continued to make and sell variations on the theme for the next two years.

Once Max had started the play group funded by Social Services at Wallace House in Oat Street I made contact with the administrative team and through this contact heard of a job – another cleaning job but at least it would fit in with the time I had available. Following an interview I was offered the post which involved cleaning The Oak Room on two mornings a week. The Oak Room was a solidly panelled meeting room behind a classical facade on the High Street and backed onto a complex of offices at Wallace House. On two evenings a week I also cleaned these Social Services Offices. Once again I was able to top up our joint income so we could buy some extras for the house.

On another morning I would go to Swan Lane School where Dylan was a pupil and listen in turn to children from the second and third year doing their reading practice. Dylan was reading well by now; when he was three years old I had started him on the flash-card system recommended by Glen Dolan and now he could tackle quite difficult words. Not everyone in his class had made such good progress and I enjoyed helping them with their easy readers.

My old friend Dave Woods had married in 1969 and he and his wife Wendy had their first child, Cheryl, in 1974. I felt very proud when they asked me to be a god parent. Most weeks I would drive the four miles over to South Littleton to visit Wendy for a cup of tea.

1974 was also tinged with sadness. Auntie Daye had a serious accident whilst driving her car near Stratford-upon-Avon and unfortunately died after a period of hospitalization.

* * * * *

It was during this comparatively stable period that the Journal Press announced that they would be selling off their stock of houses and would offer them to sitting tenants at a discount. Since moving from Bath almost three years previously our savings had been sitting in the Cheltenham and Gloucester Building Society gaining a small amount of interest. The children seemed settled and Bryn felt his job offered a steady pay packet so we accepted the chance of a free valuation for our house with a view to buying it. We were told the market value of our house was two and a half thousand pounds and the company offered a discount of five hundred pounds. We quickly did our sums and realised that with our deposit of five hundred pounds we would need a mortgage of only one and a half thousand. It meant that once again we could get our feet on the bottom rung of the housing ladder and without the trauma of moving. For once Bryn raised no objections and the purchase was soon completed.

As usual our home reflected our rather eclectic style. We were still devotees of the Art Nouveau movement and we decorated our hall with wallpaper featuring sinuous plant forms interlaced with semi nude women in the style of Alphonse Mucha and all in subdued tones of olive green and brown and wine-red. On the wall we hung a mirror in a copper frame and a print by Arthur Rackham in a delightfully designed wide wooden frame dating from the early twentieth century and depicting the iconic emblems of the Art Nouveau period. It had cost me the grand sum of two pence at a jumble sale!

Our sitting room had furniture of several styles from the 1930's to the 1960's. I had bought cheaply a drop-arm sofa in a classic Art Deco design chenille fabric and together with our period bookcases and classic sixties furniture it needed a plain background. I decided to emulate the style of a deco-period cinema and painted the walls rose pink with a wide band of wine red all round the room. For the woodwork I chose a soft deco green. I had begun to collect Art Deco pieces from jumble sales and flea markets and had acquired a pewter aeroplane tilted on a curved stand and a metal photo frame that reflected the angular stepped design of the period. These sat on the mantelpiece each side of a reproduction 1930's style chrome clock.

I loved our home and enjoyed working in it which seemed to contradict the beliefs of the Women's Movement and I felt ambivalent about my need for a domestic order and framework of chores. I thought it was strange that I would feel content when our lives were so conventional and predictable. Shouldn't I have felt rebellious?

Max was going now to a regular playgroup at Bengeworth which Dylan had previously attended for two years. I had admired the way they planned their activities throughout the three-hour session each morning and had felt very confident at leaving Dylan in their care. Max's behaviour was a little calmer now and he responded well to the alternating programme of physical activity, and mental stimulation.

First of all the children would take part in a free-for-all to let off steam riding round the room on tricycles, pedal cars, or scooters or maybe push a doll's pram round or bowl a hoop. Once all the equipment had been put away the children were glad to split into groups for a quiet learning period where they might do jigsaws or colour pictures and the older ones would learn to write or tell the time. After milk and biscuits when the children sat on tiny chairs it was time for playing in small groups and learning to share. Water play with jugs and bottles around a plastic pool or digging in the sand pit were very popular but some of them preferred playing shops or keeping house and sometimes a small group would practice throwing and catching a ball. By the time their parents came for them at twelve o'clock the children were gathered in a semi-circle on the floor listening with rapt attention to a story and wouldn't notice their parents jostling in the porch to try and see through the half-glazed doors.

In August 1976 my oldest friend Sylvia married Brian. We had spent our childhood together and she was chief bridesmaid at my wedding. At Christmas 1973 she had returned from her nursing job in the Ivory Coast, West Africa and although we met less frequently now, she written to tell me about the love she had found and of the plans for her marriage.

That September I decided I would sign on for an evening class. It was years since I had been to keep fit and badminton but I fancied learning a new craft and eventually selected pottery from the adult education brochure. It was the highlight of my week and I delighted in learning all the ways of making a pot. Before we were allowed on the potter's wheel there were other techniques to perfect.

The most basic of these was a thumb pot and it felt prehistoric to shape the oozing clay into a ball then push your thumb into the centre, gently working the hole bigger and the wall of the pot thinner and finally flattening the bottom so it would stand up level. I remembered the times as a child when I had begged a spadeful of clay from Dad as he dug out the fishpond in the corner of the garden. Twenty years ago I had baked these basic pots in the oven and painted them with poster paint but now I learnt to use a proper glaze before they were fired in the kiln.

The next stage was making a coil pot where the idea was to roll long even slippery snakes of clay and coil them round to build up the sides of a pot on a flat base. As the pot became taller you smeared the inside of the pot smooth with a wet finger and the shape could be built out wider or narrowed to a thin neck. We looked through books for ideas on how to decorate our pots with a textured finish and were surprised when our tutor showed us how to achieve these with a stick or spatula.

We were all itching to move on to the wheel but there was always a queue where the more experienced class members waited impatiently for their turn to throw their dollop of clay. We had to bide our time and wait for our turn and meanwhile there was a chance to make slab pots. After thorough kneading to obtain an even texture the knobs of clay were rolled out with a domestic rolling pin and cut into shapes with a scraper blade. It was important to have some idea of the finished shape you were trying to achieve, whether square, cylindrical, oval or something more exotic like a heart. Firstly you cut a base of the right size then the walls of the pot; then it remained to smear diluted clay or 'slip' along the joints to hold it together and seal the edges. Design experience soon built up once you had a pile of collapsed pots on your bench that were the wrong proportions to support their sides!

Eventually the longed-for time would arrive and we were shown how to sit astride the mucky damp kick-wheel. The waiting students howled with laughter if a blob of badly positioned clay flew off into the deep bowl surrounding the wheel. Getting the rhythm of the leg movements to propel the wheel was a real challenge and often it would start to turn the wrong way. After many attempts we became adept at centring our clay and working it up with our cupped hands and back down with the heel of our hand until the slimy lump was ready to shape. Over the next couple of terms we all managed to take our turn on the wheel and then the best students progressed to the electrically operated wheel.

Finally when our efforts came out of the kiln it was time to apply the glaze and sometimes we painted a simple picture or a squiggly design and sometimes with the tutor's assistance learnt how to do a pattern in a coloured slip glaze. I enjoyed pottery classes so much that I signed up for a further two sessions and proudly presented my efforts as presents. One evening I made a name plate for our house with *Clinton Villa* in a raised coil of script and two screw holes made by poking a pencil through the clay.

Some Saturdays Bryn would be asked to do four hours of overtime but usually the weekends were for leisure and we would follow our old habit of driving to a city to look round the shops. We both liked to keep abreast of the latest ideas in design, both in fashion and interiors. One year Bryn bought me a paper dress fastened on the shoulders by tape and depicting a larger-than-life head and shoulders photo of Bob Dylan. Usually at some stage Bryn would make for a record shop and I would take the children to a park or museum. His knowledge of jazz was impressive and each month he would assimilate more facts gleaned from magazines. He now corresponded with even more people in the UK and across the world and discussed the possibility of trying to get a freelance job writing articles or reviewing records. He loved discussing compositions, styles and interpretations but although I had now been listening to jazz for ten years I couldn't talk about it on the intellectual level that Bryn wanted.

On Sundays we usually went for a drive round the lanes and villages of the Vale of Evesham.

'Oh, no! Not more cabbage fields!' Bryn would groan. 'Hell, it's so flat and boring.'

'I find it very calming,' I replied. 'There are so many different shades of green in the crops,' I recalled as I visualized the blue-green of the winter cabbage and the bright green of the spring onions.

'If it's not cabbages it's beans or asparagus,' he argued. 'There's nothing to break it up.'

'Of course there is! Look at the pretty villages and the black and white houses,' I countered, pointing at a cluster of half-timbered buildings as we drove through The Lenches, a series of delightful villages between Evesham and Inkberrow. 'Think of all the history behind the doors. There's such a sense of continuity,' I continued enthusiastically.

'You mean people who have never travelled the sixteen miles to Cheltenham?' Bryn queried incredulously. 'I shall never get used to this area, it even smells different.'

I knew I would never win this debate: from the very start Bryn had not taken to this area. The surrounding hills of Malvern, Bredon, the Lickeys and the Cotswolds made the county just about bearable but he said he missed the sea and the rugged grandeur of the moors.

'Shall we call in to see Steve and Maggie?' I asked. 'We could cadge a cup of tea.'

'OK, I suppose so, Bryn replied unenthusiastically.

We quite often called on the off-chance with varying degrees of welcome. My brother and his wife both worked full time and travelled quite a distance to work; this meant they had to get up early on a week day so they relished a quiet, relaxed weekend and I don't think two adventurous children were always welcome!

In addition I had noticed from other family get-togethers that there seemed a sense of disapproval about how we dealt with our sons. Often, when we were in company it seemed a better option, for a quiet life, to lower my standards and just let things go but I felt that family members judged us and found us guilty of too lax an approach. In any case there seemed little point in imposing a threat that we were unable to fulfil when we were in company so I felt it was better to let minor misdemeanours pass unchecked rather than create a scene or lose face. Sometimes when I decided to be strict Bryn would give way to the children's demands and I would feel embarrassed at our lack of consistency.

Occasionally Bryn would begin talking about one of the taboo subjects – mainly politics and I could feel the strain in the atmosphere developing. He seemed oblivious – unless he was being deliberately provocative – and would pass from politicians, to the unions and strikes and then on to the usual debate about the class war and the difference between the 'haves and have-nots.' Once the topic moved on to social reform and Bryn's belief that everyone should have equal opportunities or even drop out of the system I could see disapproving glances being exchanged and I knew we had lost ground. If the subject shifted to immigrants or gypsies or others classed as skivers, people discreetly moved away or went to make a drink and Bryn would finally wind down. I felt proud that he stood up for his beliefs and could hold his own in a discussion but knew it was pointless to persuade my family and friends from their own opinions and at worst I knew it would alienate us even further.

I loved the changing seasons and looked out for the milestones of country life. The migrant workers bundled up in waterproof coats and headscarves would sit in the fields on upturned wooden crates bunching up spring onions. Later in the year we might see these resilient men and women planting potatoes, four abreast on a platform at the back of a tractor, deftly dropping the chitted tuber into the furrows. Sprout picking looked a miserable job and often in the worst of the weather standing with their backs to sheeting rain the pickers would strip the stalks and toss the knobbly sprouts into a box.

After the heavy spring rains I would drive round looking at the flood water and compare it to previous years, noting the level on the marker posts rammed into the river banks. Then as the year progressed I would drive Mum round the blossom trail in the Vale of Evesham. Sometimes we would encounter a coach full of sightseers on a bend in the lane; it had become a seasonal ritual for visitors from Birmingham to come and admire the orchards of white and pink blossom stretching for miles.

We lived in our two-bedroomed house in Kings Road for almost six years until finally it was no longer convenient for Dylan and Max to share a room and we decided in 1976 to look for a larger home.

Chapter 6

 Princess Road, Evesham

At first glance our new house was not very different from our old one: still the traditional Midlands red brick and the dark grey slate roof and still the same small front garden the statutory six feet deep and fronting the row of houses built at the very beginning of the twentieth century. A low wall had once been topped by railings.

A second look revealed that this house had bay windows, both top and bottom and the brickwork was broken up by a slab of rough-cast render. The sloping road had a nice feel to it; at the top there was a gravelly track which led to a big 1930's villa and several acres of orchards and we had noticed when we had first viewed the house that the fruit trees came up almost to the back fence and formed a pink and white mosaic of blossom.

When we had arrived on the doorstep clutching our estate agent's particulars an elderly lady had ushered us in with a welcome, opening the wide front door to reveal a coloured tile floor. She had led the way along the hall, past panelled doors all covered in thick brown varnish and past the staircase with its fancy banisters to the kitchen door. As she held the brass door knob in her hand she turned to us, saying over her shoulder,

'See those yellow slip mats by all the doors and the long runner? Well, I made all those myself, working the cut wool into canvas. Look – the stair carpet too.'

We showed due surprise and admired her handiwork.

'They have years more wear in them even though it's several decades since I made them. I'll leave them for you; I won't need them in my new bungalow. There are hearth rugs in the downstairs rooms too.'

She had dipped down two steps into the kitchen and we followed her into the old fashioned room. Opposite the door was a deep alcove with a high shelf topping the lintel. In the opening a gas stove had replaced the range and we noticed the chrome taps all neatly turned down to the off position but the grey and white enamel was spattered with signs of cooking. Screwed under the pitch-pine shelf was a brass rail where a tea towel and floor cloth hung to dry next to a pair of bloomers.

It was obvious that the old lady spent a lot of time in the kitchen: the scrubbed table in the middle of the quarry tiled floor was ready for the next meal and an elm chair was pulled out.

'Would you like a cup of tea while I tell you about the house?' she had asked us, taking the lid off the aluminium kettle to fill it from the high tap over the shallow brown crock sink.

Our eyes swept round the painted brick walls and took in the tall kitchen cabinet and the wooden draining board under the sash window then we watched as she reached the tea caddy from the shelf where it sat next to the clock and spooned the leaves into a brown pot.

'I've been widowed a long time now,' she began, 'but my husband bought this house when it was newly built and he had just married his first wife.' She poured in the boiling water, stirred the pot and arranged the striped tea-cosy before taking cups and saucers from the cabinet. 'When she died he married me and we had some good years together but I'm from Devon and now this place is too big for me I'm going to a bungalow in Paignton.'

We stood back as she moved round the table to open a door which exposed a big pantry where she kept a bottle of milk on the wooden shelves.

'Let's go into the front room for our tea,' she suggested, loading everything onto a wooden tray with ornate brass handles. She led us back along the hall and as she pushed the door open we noticed an art-nouveau-design finger plate tacked above the knob. Bryn nudged me and we exchanged glances thinking how beautiful our furniture would look in this un-renovated house which was virtually the same as when it had been built.

We sat on a faded settee and looked admiringly towards the fire-place where green marble panels decorated a slate surround and dark green ceramic tiles with an embossed art nouveau motif sloped in towards a cast iron grate.

'This room catches the afternoon sun,' our elderly hostess told us. 'I let the blinds down after lunch.'

We glanced over to the wide-angled bay window where frayed and rotting cords hung from the drooping wooden slats of the louvered blinds.

'Have your tea and I'll show you the rest of the house.' It was obvious that she was making the most of her visitors and we knew Bryn would be late back to work.

'We can only spare another ten minutes,' I had explained. 'Maybe we could come back on Saturday with the children?'

'I'd like that but just let me show you the dining room,' she insisted, putting down her cup and saucer and making for the door.

The back room had long windows that opened onto blue-brick steps leading down to the yard and overlooking the garden. Another fireplace provided the focal point but this one was embellished in wine-red marble and the maroon tiled hearth was surrounded by a low fender. The high picture rail encircling the room supported some old speckled paintings and it too was varnished in dark brown to match the architraves and skirting boards.

Once outside we had little time to exchange views.

'I've got to get back to work as fast as I can,' Bryn had muttered as he swung his bike round to face downhill. 'We'll talk about it tonight but I really like it.'

'So do I,' I shouted after his disappearing back.

That evening we discussed not only the house but its location on the lower eastern slopes of Greenhill. A grid of four roads had been established around the end of the nineteenth century and the houses were well built and were conveniently close to the town centre with the railway station little over five minutes walk away. Prince Henry's Grammar School faced the bottom of Princess Road although it had now become the senior school in a tripartite comprehensive system. Alongside the school was a track that led round the orchards to footpaths across open fields and gave access to riverside meadows.

We had returned to the house on Saturday with the children in tow and feeling that before the day was out we would firm up the interest we had registered with the estate agent by making an offer for the house.

The smiling owner had taken the children into the back garden and shown them her rhubarb which she fed daily with household scraps. The inanimate plant didn't hold their interest and they looked towards us doubtfully.

'What's behind these doors?' I asked.

The first one was opened to reveal a high-level iron cistern eight feet above a thick ceramic pan topped by a wooden seat.

'So useful if you are in the garden,' our guide had ventured. 'It will be convenient when the children are playing out here.'

Lifting the thumb latch on the other door she stepped aside for us to admire the cavernous coal house and the sun glinted on massive lumps of coal that would need a sledge hammer to break them up.

'Room for bicycles and garden tools in here, dearie,' she informed us pointing to a shed tucked into the corner of the yard. 'And just round here is the side gate leading to the passage that you share with next door. Wipe your feet well and we'll go upstairs.'

Although elderly she had nipped up the thickly carpeted staircase and paused on the landing for the four of us to catch up.

'There is a smaller bedroom over the kitchen and another one overlooking the fields,' she told us, glancing at the two boys. 'The biggest room is at the front; come and have a look.'

We had admired the room, well lit by the bay window and mentally assessed it for space to fit our furniture.

'I've got something to suggest, my dears,' the old lady said conspiratorially. 'I won't need all this big furniture in my new bungalow and if you have the house I would like to leave it for you. There's the big wardrobe with the mirror and the dressing table over there,' she indicated with a gesture. 'They are good solid pieces and well made. No wood-worm either.'

We had nodded our appreciation and moved on to the bathroom. This was the most disappointing room in the house. At least it wouldn't be cold! The bath took up half the floor space with the geyser bolted onto the wall above and somehow the wash basin and toilet were pushed in on the other side. It was fine as long as you sat with your feet tucked under the bath when you used the facilities!

Once we had said our goodbyes Bryn had driven down the road before we both spoke at once. We thought the house would be just right for us, our possessions and our lifestyle. Our collections of books, records and bric-a-brac would fit in and blend seamlessly with the surroundings. I hadn't been looking forward to moving from the suburb of Bengeworth and all my friends but now I had no regrets and was already formulating colour schemes and decorating ideas. After our two visits I knew where all our furniture would be placed for maximum effect.

Now, it was removal day and we felt like old hands at it: this was our sixth move since we had married eleven years ago in1965. In hardly any time at all the furniture was installed in the places I had mentally allocated. The only two pieces that didn't look at home were our modern purchases – the canvas butterfly chair and the inflated black plastic seat and to be honest neither of them was supremely comfortable. We decided to get rid of them and concentrate on more traditional furniture, but for now they would have to stay.

The school summer holidays were soon upon us and our boys had plenty of children to play with. A few doors up the road lived Margaret who had been in the bed next to me in Avonside Maternity Hospital when Dylan was born. Two sons had joined Karen who was two days older than Dylan and I was delighted to have a ready-made family of friends. Down the road in a bigger, double-fronted house lived Kate with her husband and four sons and several days a week us three mothers would join up for walks, picnics and excursions or sit drinking tea while our combined tribe of nine children played in tents or sandpits, or on swings and bikes. Sometimes we would walk across the back-fields and scramble up the embankment of the disused railway line that had formerly carried trains from Redditch and Alcester to Ashchurch, near Tewkesbury. From this vantage point we could see the line of willow trees that marked the banks of the River Avon and turning round could identify our houses along Princess Road.

Bryn seemed better too until once again he became disenchanted with the Journal Press and decided to go for a job at Sharps the other printers in town. It didn't take very long to realise he preferred his old job and luckily his tolerant boss accepted him back.

Once the new school year had started and Dylan was back at Swan Lane School and Max had returned to his excellent playgroup we were able to make some plans for the future. We decided to invite Bryn's mother for Christmas that year – we had regularly imposed on her for our annual holidays, now it was time to play host. The trouble was, where to sleep her? The children had a room each so it would have to be downstairs but we no longer had our convertible studio couch. I looked at the Habitat catalogue to see if we could afford a long sofa bed and thought they looked such a simple design that I may be able to make one.

I noticed woodwork classes being offered down at Prince Henrys as part of the adult education prospectus and decided to enrol.

'Now, how many of you have had any woodwork experience?' the tutor asked the semi circle of students ranged round him on the grooved and pitted benches in the school workshop. 'Hmnn, not many. How many of you can use tools?'

I was the only woman there amidst about ten men and I felt nervous of raising my hand. I tentatively lifted it dreading being singled out.

'I'd better spend this first lesson showing you the tools and how they are used,' he continued, ignoring me. 'There are some magazines over there; while I am taking small groups you can scour them for ideas of what to make and we will talk about the designs next week.'

I dare not tell him that in the pocket of my jeans was a pencil drawing complete with measurements of the bed-settee I wanted to make before Christmas. The following week he moved round the class discussing plans for coffee tables and bookshelves or for the less adventurous students spice racks and chopping boards. I was greeted with an incredulous look of amazement when I produced my drawing.

'I've always been practical,' I stammered, 'and I've made several other things. I learnt how to use tools in my Dad's workshop and then I worked on a farm using machinery.'

He took the drawing and bent over it with his glasses on the end of his nose. 'Well, actually it looks pretty sound. I would make one adjustment for strength but that's all. Trouble is have we got the wood and could we store it here while you work on it?'

'I really need this piece of furniture,' I faltered. 'It would be gone from the workshop by Christmas.'

'OK, let's go and look in the storeroom and if I've got the length you can start marking it out.'

Over the next ten weeks I worked on my settee frame making two simple H-frames using mortice and tenon joints. These were joined by four six-foot-long rails and then I began planing the slats that would support the seat and back cushions. The furniture was taking shape and I thought it was time to order the high-density foam for the upholstery. In between my classes I stitched the simple covers in blue and black wool check and eased them over the blocks of foam ready to be placed on the wooden frame. On the third week in December Bryn walked down to meet me after the last session of the term. We struggled up Princess Road with the finished, varnished frame which bore a strong likeness to the one in the catalogue. We pushed it into place in the front room and arranged the cushions tailored to fit exactly between the arms. It was ready! Bryn's mother would have somewhere to sleep! The following week I made up the bed with sheets and pillowcases ready for her arrival.

In the spring term I made a record cabinet from the old beech benches that had been dismantled from the science laboratory. It was a very simple design with two long shelves thirteen inches apart – the perfect size for LPs. Bryn's collection had long since outgrown the whitewood cabinet on its spindly legs and he had resorted to storing his record collection in wooden crates so this new piece of furniture was a welcome addition.

During the week I was able to use the car for excursions into the surrounding countryside, sometimes to visit friends, sometimes on my own just for the pleasure of driving. I had become absorbed by the topography of the area and the local building styles. I had bought several books about the landscape of Britain, the changing countryside through the seasons and journeys through Britain and I felt I wanted to explore my own area.

Travelling south-east from Evesham brought me to the escarpment of the Cotswold Hills and I soon became familiar with Broadway with its world-famous wide street, Chipping Campden and its delightful market house and the other beautiful villages nestling in the lee of the hills. I memorised the tracery of lanes crossing the plateau and could soon picture the places that each lane led to. The huge fields were a sea of corn which changed from pea green to tawny cream as the seasons progressed and the quintessential mellow gold of the local stone added another texture to the vibrant landscape. The high stony grasslands supported sheep that gave the Cotswolds its wealth.

Down on the plain the lightly wooded Vale of Evesham stretched across towards the Malvern Hills broken only by the pimple of Bredon Hill and the tower of Tewkesbury Abbey. The lush well-watered meadows of the Avon and Severn produced good grass and ash and willow trees featured strongly in this soft green landscape. The fields were edged with hawthorn and black thorn and along the lanes were spinneys of oak and hazel where a pheasant might sometimes break cover. Here the local stone was not suitable for construction purposes and the houses and barns were either of brick or picturesque wooden-framed buildings with the spaces between the timbers in-filled with brick or wattle and daub.

In the school holidays I would take the children and we might visit Pershore, loved for its marvellous toy shop or take a picnic to a river-bank or pick blackberries.

At weekends Saturday was spent in the time-honoured way with Bryn by a trip to the shops of Worcester or Cheltenham or preferably Birmingham or Gloucester. We had established a pattern for these trips and once we had done the rounds of the clothes shops we ate our sandwiches and drank our flask of coffee. Bryn would make tracks for a record shop buying a magazine on the way and I would usher the boys into the nearest swing-park and try and keep them occupied for an hour or so.

Mum loved us to visit her whenever possible but she made little concession for two boisterous children in her beautifully furnished and decorated flat. Her other four grandchildren seemed to sit demurely on the sofa sipping their orange squash but Dylan and Max soon began to poke each other and Mum would suggest we gave them a good slap.

The flat was a haven of tranquillity and fresh seasonal flowers from Mum's garden were always in evidence. She had planted two cherry trees in the municipal lawn surrounding the flats, much to the annoyance of the man driving the gang-mower and when she added rambling roses growing up a secure post she had to agree to trim the grass herself round the plants. Within a couple of years she had dug up a yard of turf round the trees and planted it with bulbs and perennials. The flowery bank rose steeply outside her window so despite being on the first floor she had a good view of her patch from the sofa.

In the summer we sometimes drove over to Redditch to collect Mum for a fruit picking foray into the Vale of Evesham, famous for its produce. We would head for the pick-your-own fruit farms and Mum wouldn't be happy until she had punnets of strawberries or raspberries to make jam or plums and damsons later in the year. What we couldn't pick we bought from the fruit stalls dotted all round the Vale. Sacks of shallots were needed for pickling to eat at Christmas and anything else on offer would be processed for Mum's freezer.

Since moving from our big family home Mum had been forced to give up making wine but I had taken over in a small way and kept a few demi-johns of yeasty fruit bubbling away until it had finished working. I learnt from Mum that most fruit or vegetables could be transformed into a potent wine and under her guidance I learnt how to brew plum, damson and apple wine, and use dandelions, elderflowers and lime blossom to create fragrant and alcoholic drinks. The root vegetables produced wine for the dedicated imbiber as the rather woody flavour wasn't to everyone's taste but potatoes, carrots, beetroot and parsnips could all be used. Best of all was the fruit for free that we would pick from the hedgerows; elderberries, rosehips, wild plums and sloes. Over the months of the early winter I would bottle it ready to offer a glass at family gatherings.

We were feeling settled in our home in Princess Road and everything seemed to be falling into place. I had started going to church again and the boys attended Sunday school. Years ago I had decided against having them christened because it seemed hypocritical when we weren't regular church goers but now I hoped that by attending they would reinforce the moral values I had tried to instil at home. Bryn was a reluctant participant but came along with us to set a good example. I needed to find a task I could do to fulfil my Christian social commitment and finally decided to offer my artistic services to design a weekly poster announcing the topic of the Sunday service and the name of the preacher and on a separate sheet I outlined the week's activities.

* * * * *

Two years had passed quickly and we had turned this faded house into a stylish home with some period-design wallpaper and borders and my growing collection of ceramics and collectables. Bryn would help me to paper the walls, a skill he had learnt from observing his mother but essentially he was not much of an odd-jobber and plastering, tiling, drilling and fixing usually fell to me. My mother would reinforce his ineptitude by comparing him to Dad.

'Doesn't he look clumsy with a hammer in his hand?' she would comment. 'I can see you are itching to snatch it from him and do the job yourself.'

'Oh well, he tries, I suppose,' I would grudgingly sigh, trying to be loyal, but she had hit the nail on its head!

'We need Dad here for this; it would soon be done – and properly!' she snapped.

I had begun to explore junk shops in every town we visited in the hope of adding to my collection of art-nouveau bits and pieces but I noticed that items of hand painted art-pottery dating from the 1930s had started to filter into the shops. Often given as stylish wedding presents fifty years previously their owners were now finding them outmoded and would no longer give them cupboard space.

I loved these pieces of china, brightly painted with flowers or trees, birds or cottages. I had bought up oddments here and there; a couple of saucers, a fruit dish or a bread and butter plate and my collection gradually extended to include quirky items decorated with violent colours in abstract patterns. No-one else seemed to see the attraction and friends and family alike thought I was barmy to proudly put these ceramics on my dresser.

I had been to a second year of woodwork classes and made Bryn a large cabinet for his model soldiers. To give maximum view of its contents it had plate-glass doors which slid along a rebate I had cut in the frame. Bryn was making a different size of models now; they were based on the six-inch Airfix figures of famous historical people but he would hack them about and convert them to perhaps a Samurai or a Greek Hoplite warrior all in a perfect replica of their uniforms cunningly made from metal, fabric and cardboard.

My final attempt at woodwork had been a desk for Dylan's birthday. It had a sloping hinged flap that hid the storage cubby-holes and a bookshelf underneath and I think I was more pleased with it than Dylan was!

The summer of 1978 had passed and Max was old enough to enrol at Evesham Primary school in Swan Lane. He was already quite advanced in his learning skills but because of his low attention span his teachers often set him individually selected work and kept a close eye on him for signs of mood swings.

Dylan had been kitted out in his uniform for St Egwins Middle School and the week before term started had his photograph taken in his grey jumper and striped tie. I desperately hoped both our sons would do well; we had tried to give them all the chances we could – visits to museums, castles, and galleries and always lots of books – as many as they could read, and lots of conversation, never avoiding the dozens of questions they fired at us. I cast my mind back to my own childhood and remembered the chemistry set I had for one Christmas and the brass microscope Dad had kept for me from his own youth. We didn't have many books in the house but there was always a sense of curiosity being fulfilled and discussions about the universe and the meaning of life.

Dylan and Max outside the french windows, 1978.

I too was expanding my understanding and that autumn I signed on for a two year A-level, day-release course in Sociology.

Although I'd been to courses in Yoga and keep-fit, then pottery and woodwork I hadn't studied an academic subject since I had left college in 1964 and I was excited by the idea of getting down to a serious topic. The venue for the class was an annexe of Evesham College in a village just outside the town and I hoped it would be possible to walk there. I didn't relish the idea of a trudge along the main road to Pershore but after poring over a map I realised there was another way to reach Hampton and I devised an unusual route and decided to test it out. One Sunday before the start of term I set off accompanied by Bryn and the children. We walked the length of the High

Street and continued down Vine Street as far as Merstow Green where ten years previously I had worked at the vets. In a corner of the gravelly open space was a narrow, largely unknown lane leading to the River Avon. Alongside the rutted road was an ancient wall that five hundred years ago had formed a boundary of Evesham Abbey land. The fields each side were market gardens and I smiled at the contrast – on the left were spring onions and on the right chrysanthemums!

At the bottom of the lane we faced a choppy expanse of the river and across the water saw the ferryman's house. An ancient chain-ferry had existed here for hundreds of years and a notice told us to hail the ferryman on the other side. The long flat-bottomed boat cast off and the man hauled on the chain that was hanging across the river and gradually drew the craft closer to our bank. Stepping in and paying our few pennies fare we settled down for the crossing noticing that the wind cut across the water when we were mid-river.

Reaching the far side we helped the children out and walked through the cottage garden and onto a footpath that led along the edge of Clarke's Hill past a caravan site to the road where I had identified the college building in what looked like an industrial estate. What an adventure it would be, arriving at college like that! Going home I timed the walk and checked that the ferry ran daily then I made my final decision to sign up for the course.

The lectures were absolutely fascinating and each week I looked forward to covering a new topic on the syllabus as we progressed through demographics and family structure; crime, law and order; education; and class, wealth and poverty. Our tutor Fiona had a way of making the subject live and her enthusiasm transmitted to us. I bought new text books, particularly the affordable Pelican series and ordered others from the library.

We discussed women in society and I linked the theory with the subjects I had read about in Spare Rib magazine. After each session a knot of women would hang back to engage Fiona in feminist topics.

Most of the class were mature students who hadn't taken an exam for years and we wondered how we would manage in the advanced level paper. We opted to take GCE ordinary level at the end of the first year even though we hadn't covered all the subjects yet – at least it would break us in gently to the discipline of sitting a formal exam. In July 1979 our results were published and we had all passed with good grades and with relief we signed on for a second year.

Fired up with enthusiasm I also enrolled for a new ten week evening course in Cheltenham called *Women in Literature* run by the Workers Education Association. It was a real effort to drive sixteen miles, often in bad weather, but the course was so rewarding that I didn't regret it and it ended up by altering my life.

I parked the car under the trees in the crescent of Regency houses by the bus station and scanned the sign-boards for the WEA centre. Climbing the stairs I felt apprehensive and anxious; I didn't know anyone else on this course and I wondered if they would all be very middle-class leaving me feeling the odd-one-out or perhaps they all had degrees and I would be intellectually out of my depth. I crowded into a room with a dozen or so other women and waited for the tutor to address the class.

'Jane Austen, Iris Murdoch, Charlotte Brontë, Colette, Daphne du Maurier,' fifteen minutes later our collective voices rang out across the room in response to our tutor's question about what women authors we had read.

'I'm going to pass round a reading list,' she said. 'Take one and pass the rest on.'

As the sheets were circulated we scrutinised the titles but most of them were new to me.

'Each week we'll take a different author and discuss her best known novel. We can talk about her subject matter and how she looks at it from a woman's perspective. We'll analyse her writing style and compare it to other books she has written and to other authors in the same genre.'

Some of the class were scribbling on their note pads and some were leaning back in their uncomfortable chairs listening with concentration.

'Of course, I'd like you to read as many of the books as you can; obviously it will make for a more meaningful discussion. If you don't have time to read a book a week then try to scan it and get the gist of how that author writes. What you don't read during the ten week course you can follow up later.'

My mind flicked over to life at home: two lively children, two part-time jobs, a house to run, a demanding mother to placate – how could I read a book a week?

The tutor's voice cut across my thoughts as she suggested that someone should name a book that we could discuss now and soon we were all making a contribution to the discussion with our feelings about subject matter, style, pace and grammatical devices. Words that I had never articulated were surfacing from my subconscious and I found I had the confidence to add my own comments about the book we were discussing. The atmosphere of the class felt safe and non-competitive and my fears of not fitting in were quickly forgotten.

By the time I had driven the sixteen miles back to Evesham I felt tired but I also experienced a feeling of intense excitement as if I was opening up a new world where imagination could run hand in hand with understanding. Bryn was watching the television when I let myself into the house at nine thirty, but he switched off and offered me a coffee as I passed him the typed sheet of book titles.

'You're going to have your work cut out, reading this lot,' he shrugged, casting his eyes over the little known names: Erica Jong, Doris Lessing, Anais Nin, Virginia Woolf and the rest. 'Where will you get them from?'

'If I can't buy my own copy the library may order it for me,' I assumed. 'Really I would like to build up my own collection of women's literature so perhaps I can ask for some for Christmas and buy some out of my spending money.'

Over the next ten weeks my mind was fermenting with a heady brew of concepts and clichés, morals and metaphors. In my spare time I was engrossed in the books I was reading my way through and reflected on the insights made more obvious by the talent and perception of our tutor.

Each week after the class had ended a group of women would remain behind to try and extract a deeper meaning from the feelings externalised in a particular book. We felt we wanted to carry the discussion further and decided to meet up in Cheltenham one day. As the weeks passed and our extra literature discussion group developed we found that we were discussing more than books. Most of the half-dozen or do women had read *Spare Rib* magazine at some stage and had come across the term consciousness raising and this is what our closely knit, safe group of like-minded women developed into: a consciousness raising group.

Although I was enjoying a very exciting and positive phase in my personal life things were not going very well in my family life.

Once again Bryn had started to find fault with the Journal Press and regularly trawled through the situations vacant columns of his NGA union newspaper.

'Shall I try for this job in Frome?' he would question. 'They are a very prestigious company and the quality of the books they produce is excellent.'

'Do we really want to live in Frome?' I had sighed.

'What about Chippenham then, there's a place there. Look, Bath too – that place along the Bristol Road,' he enthused.

We had been through this so often over the years that I was fed up with it and decided to give him no encouragement. He'd already tried the rival company in Evesham for a few months.

'I can't stick it much longer. It's driving me mad', he continued.

I didn't want to move; things were going well. I had two new circles of friends, one a set of neighbours and mothers and the other group were people I met at my classes. I had worked hard on the house and it was looking up-together and stylish. The garden had come into its own now, especially as I had filled window boxes and hanging baskets and planted a few rows of vegetables. No! I didn't want to move and wished that Bryn felt more content.

Two weeks later he said,

'I'd like to drive down to Cirencester this weekend and suss it out. If it looks OK I may apply for a machine manager's job there.'

Angie outside number 22.

I had swallowed down my words thinking at least the Cotswolds might be nicer than Wiltshire and replied with a nonchalant 'OK'.

Cirencester was an attractive town but a glance into the estate agents' windows confirmed that house prices were steep. Bryn seemed set on his idea and wrote his letter of application listing all the printing offices he had worked for. I had told myself to keep calm, it might not happen but he was offered the job and gave notice at The Journal.

The plan was for him to settle into lodgings and look for a suitable house for us to buy. He would send the particulars to me and we could all go down to view any nice houses. Two weeks later we had all waved him off with hugs and kisses and I waited for his first letter. Six weeks later he had decided that neither the job nor the town were for him and asked for his old job back.

'Perhaps we can just move out of Evesham,' he had continued the same old gripe. 'It's so parochial, nothing ever happens, there's no culture and all people talk about is growing things,' he exaggerated.

'I think you expect too much. You've got your friend Tony to talk to about films and Malcolm to discuss politics with and you see people at film society. Then there are all the people you write to,' I had reminded him.

'Would you consider moving to Cheltenham, Angie,' he asked me.

'Hmnn, possibly, but could we afford a house there?' I questioned. 'I like the style of the older period houses but they might be out of our range, and where would you work?'

Most of the second half of 1978 had been spent looking at a dozen or so houses in Cheltenham but nothing else had moved forward. Bryn switched his interest to Worcester and 1979 was taken over by a feverish spate of viewing another dozen places. We had eventually found one we liked, a Regency house in a delightful walk of similar period homes. It was near the Diglis basin and access to the canal and river as well as the city centre. I could see myself living here; it had style and period features; our stuff would look good. I liked the enormous kitchen in the basement with the ceiling supported on two huge cast iron columns and the look of the old sofa in the corner and the flagstone floor. We didn't get round to having a survey: Bryn developed cold feet. I think he remembered our experiences in Bath as he looked doubtfully at the kitchen ceiling and mentally listed all the potential hazards, both financial and practical. Our house hunting had stopped for the time being.

Other difficulties developed: Bryn would sit with the Sunday colour supplement on his lap looking dejected, and wallow in self pity.

'There's no one for me to talk to. I'm starved of culture. All I want is someone to listen to jazz with and maybe discuss a track on an album,' he would grizzle, moodily.

'For heaven's sake!' I expostulated. 'No one's going to come to you! You'll have to do what I've done and go out and make friends. See if there's a jazz appreciation society in Cheltenham or something,' I continued, not wanting him to winge on any longer.

'As if I can do that when I come home from work, I just want to collapse,' was his excuse.

'Well what are you going on about then?' I retorted with my exasperation mounting. 'Just do something! Stick a postcard in a shop window and ask for jazz fans.' I felt at the end of my tether.

The next day while Bryn was at work I roughed out the wording on a card and suggested putting one in the paper shop and one on the display case outside the Central Market.

'You've got nothing to lose,' I reasoned optimistically. 'You might get a reply,' I added asserting my positive personality.

Ten days later the first call came; someone in town would enjoy listening to records with Bryn as long as he could be home early – he was a postman.

A few days after that the telephone rang again; a woman this time. She lived in a village half way to Cheltenham but would love to meet up for a jazz session. Bryn couldn't believe it! He made arrangements for them to call round one evening and friendships developed that were to last for many years.

* * * * *

In 1979 my dear Auntie Chris had a stroke and had to rest in bed for a few days. Another more serious stroke followed and I volunteered to drive over to Redditch to collect Mum so we could go to Alcester to look after her. The district nurse had made her comfortable and Mum and I took over, making Auntie some soup and gently helping to feed her. I had to return home to meet Max from School so after lunch I drove Mum home promising to collect her again the next day which was her birthday. Auntie was worse and Mum decided to stay the night. Sadly Auntie died on the seventh of March and we arranged the funeral service in the parish church.

A few days later we returned to her flat to make decisions about her things. Much of the furniture was the best of what had been in my grandparents' house and we didn't want to see it end up on the rubbish tip. I thought long and hard about whether I could give any of it house space and ended up with an oak bookcase, a couple of bedroom chairs and a chest of drawers, while Mum reclaimed a side table that she had been given as a twenty-first birthday present many years ago and a few small pieces that would fit into her flat. No one in the family wanted all the useful bits and bobs that made up a home; the bed linen, the pots and pans, the cutlery and crockery let alone the ornaments collected over the years. I thought I could store some of it in the loft or the garden shed in case it was ever needed and filled up the boot of the car to haul it back to Evesham.

I soon realised I had made a big mistake and I would have to move it on. I had noticed that once a week, in the Avon Street Produce Market, there were stalls where people sold items of second hand furniture or crafts. Once the produce had been auctioned and the scraps of cabbage leaves swept up and the crates of plums shifted out people set up their tables under the corrugated metal roof where a cold wind blew across the concrete. I had looked round once or twice on the way home from taking Max to school so I made enquiries and booked a table.

Next week I unloaded an unlikely batch of mops and buckets, cobweb brushes, dustpans, an ironing board, a pile of blankets and box of mismatched china. To make it look better I included a box of brass ornaments and perched a couple of my bright crocheted cushions on the end. By lunch time most of it was gone and I packed the boot thinking I'd done quite well. I would try it again sometime. A month later I cleared out some unwanted toys and books to add to the remaining things of Auntie's and for good measure added some clothes I didn't want. Nearly every thing was sold and I had enjoyed the banter and barter on the stall. I had got the bug! I wanted to do it again but I had nothing left to sell.

I wondered where I could buy some new stock and then I remembered – on the way home from town I had noticed sometimes that the cattle market next to the Railway Tavern was regularly taken over by a general household auction sale and the next week I ventured in. The cattle pens were swept clean and each metal enclosure contained a different lot all marked up with their numbers. By the time I arrived the auctioneer was making his way precariously along a plank balanced at the back of the pens. The jostling crowd moved along with him as he cast his eyes over the amorphous group of people, waiting for the bids. He would slap his clip board to seal the final bid as he shouted 'Sold!' and hand his full sheets to his assistant to run them to the office to have the buyers dues made up. I was fascinated by the whole process and soon forgot a newcomer's anxiety about being landed with an unwanted purchase if they scratched their nose at the wrong time!

I needed to see what was being sold and made my way over to a section they hadn't reached. I was astounded at the variety of goods being auctioned. There was good period furniture, carpets, beds, electrical goods, bicycles, tools and loads of cardboard boxes filled with the residue of someone's home – framed black and white photographs, paintings, vintage tea-sets, broken ornaments and all the rest. I believed that I could make some money if I could buy a box of assorted bric-a-brac cheaply enough. I would wash and polish, clean and mend and if necessary could upholster small pieces of furniture. I always read the collectors and antiques guide before we passed it on to Mum each month and I thought I stood a good chance of buying things that would earn me a few extra pounds. A frisson of excitement ran through my chilled body and I was hooked!

Could I take on any more? Would there be time? Walking home across the railway bridge and along the streets of terraced houses I did a mental stock-take of everything I did. I had long since given up my job cleaning the Oak Room and social services offices and replaced it with a cleaning job closer to home. Two evenings a week I would walk a short way down High Street to work my way through four floors of offices in a large property opposite Queen's Road. I washed the mugs and did the waste-paper baskets before I dusted and vacuumed all the rooms finishing up in the grotty kitchen with its sticky rings of spilt coffee and overflowing bin.

I still made cushions to sell in the cane furniture shop but I could put that on hold for a while. There were my church commitments and the posters I designed but a couple of hours a week was enough for that.

I had my housework off to a fine art with an inflexible routine of cleaning, shopping and laundry – that was the only way I could cope with it and I wasn't prepared to let my standards drop. I loved our house and was proud of everything we had done to make it look attractive; no room to manoeuvre there.

My adult education courses took another day a week and then there was my evening class which eventually was replaced by a Women's Group meeting and there was my occasional renting of a market stall. Let's see, I thought; take off the weekends which were strictly family times with the children and what was left? Not much.

My biggest new commitment was my new job as a market research interviewer. Soon after Max had started school I knew I would have to increase my input into the family budget so I had cast around for a flexible job that would fit in with school hours. Market research appeared to tick the boxes: I worked on a contract basis; the local supervisor would ring me each week to offer a new package – if I was able to do it I said yes; in school holidays I had to say no.

I had been for three days training in a hotel just outside Worcester and learnt the basics. We had to remain completely impartial as we asked questions in each section and record the answers very accurately. There were very few open-ended questions so we wouldn't need to interpret the interviewee's answers, just mark the relevant boxes. The company mainly did doorstep questionnaires rather than stop people in the street and we learnt how to launch into the questions without giving people time to back out. If they asked how long it would take we had to answer truthfully and as some research polls took over half an hour we often lost the confidence of the householder.

The main thing was to remain polite and professional at all times and we were told that the company's reputation depended on it.

Feeling less than confident I had accepted my first contract for a general survey which amalgamated a variety of topics for several different companies. My brief didn't seem very demanding but I soon learnt otherwise. To record the views of an accurate cross-section of the population the quota of the people you interviewed had to reflect the current make-up of the populace. We had learnt that people were labelled into classes according to what job they did whether high-ranking professionals, white-collar workers, or manual trades, either skilled or unskilled. At each end of the scale were people who lived on a private income and didn't work and the unemployed who existed on benefits. When it came to the practicalities of finding fifteen people in the right groups who would be willing to answer the questions it was altogether different from learning the theory. For a start we had to find eight women and seven men and then ask them what they did for a living. To complicate things the quota was subdivided into different age groups so at the end of a difficult interviewing day you might be left with, for example, one woman to find, aged twenty to thirty five who was a well-educated professional – something like a doctor or lawyer.

Surprisingly I had taken to the work with great enthusiasm and had seen it as a personal challenge to find my quota, learning quickly which part of town housed people in different socio-economic groups. I would check my questionnaires and bundle them up each week ready for posting in the special plastic wallets thinking of the pay cheque I would soon receive. Apart from that the job gave me a legitimate reason for being nosey. The householders would usually invite me in and I was endlessly fascinated by how they decorated their homes and what favourite possessions they had on display.

On alternate weeks my supervisor would try to persuade me to do a Smoking Survey asking people seemingly ridiculous questions about their cigarette preferences. I had been avidly anti-smoking for so long that I felt like I was selling my soul to the devil when I succumbed to financial temptation and accepted the contract.

So; I had reached home, my head full of thoughts, frantically trying to juggle work, study, leisure and family responsibilities. I filled the kettle and spooned coffee into a mug. Sitting at the kitchen table I felt certain that I could spare a few hours to go to the occasional auction and a few more hours to set up my stall and sell the objects I had bought. After all it wouldn't be every week.

I kept a regular check on the notices in the Evesham Journal, waiting for the next auction organised by Rightons. On the next scheduled date I dropped Max off at school and walked back up the High Street feeling a little apprehensive. The sale hadn't started but people were milling round the iron pens making notes and jotting down lot numbers. Edging my way through the crowds I unobtrusively moved closer. There were several boxes of assorted china, nothing matched but I noticed some names I recognised stamped on the underside of some plates and dishes. If I dared to make a bid that's what I would go for.

As the swirling mass of people moved closer to the lot I had identified and the auctioneer edged further along the plank of wood I felt my throat go dry. Would everyone turn and look at me? Would I look a fool? Surely they would all know this was my first time? I wasn't sure that I could go through with it. It was now or never, the lot number had been called.

'Five pounds to start me. Come on now, a good box of stuff for five pounds. No? Four?' his voice rang out across the damp air. Nobody seemed interested. 'Three then? Come on, we'll have to move on.'

'A pound,' my voice squeaked out just as the auctioneer moved away.

'Sold! Maiden bid! Name please?' he shouted across the heads of the impatient group.

I'd done it; I'd bought my first lot at an auction. I wouldn't be able to carry any more so I went up the rickety stairs to the office under the arched iron roof to hand over my coin. Feeling shaky with excitement I walked over to the cardboard box and rearranged the contents so they wouldn't clonk together then stooped down to pick it up and feeling strangely conspicuous I walked across the concrete forecourt and out of the gates with my sagging box held close to my body.

Chores forgotten I quickly ran a bowl of warm water and added a squirt of detergent. I lowered the glasses and china into the bowl and carefully washed it clean as if it was priceless Meissen. A couple of things I may as well chuck away now – the chips were too bad; no one would drink from a glass like that. One plate had a hairline crack but it was quite attractive and I thought I would keep that one on my dresser. I worked through my prizes and as I dried them I sorted out the ones I would try to sell. I would need to go back to the next auction and buy some more; then I could book another stall and start a new job as a second-hand dealer. It had a romantic ring to it and my dreams took off: I would buy something special that no-one else had noticed and sell it for hundreds; I would start a new trend for some previously neglected ceramic company; I would open a shop and become a renowned expert! For now I would content myself with being an occasional market trader.

I went back to the auction time and time again but often my purchases were destined for our own house. I bought a war-time pine dresser for a pound and enlisted Bryn's help to load it into the car boot one lunch time. Then there were two elm-seated kitchen chairs knocked down to me for fifty pence the two. I followed on with an extending pine kitchen table and Victorian iron bedsteads for the boys. Max dreaded me meeting him from school on auction day in case he had to help me lump something home. One day I bought a huge square Belgian carpet and we walked home with it rolled up and struggling to support its weight between me at the front and the two children bringing up the rear.

My collection of ceramics was growing fast, as anything that was a set, or part of one, I wanted to keep. I bought a wildly coloured Susie Cooper tea-set, willow patterned plates and pieces of blue and white-striped Cornish Ware and my dresser was soon groaning under the weight.

Our house was looking very bohemian. There was very little in it that was new and the furniture was an eclectic mix of different styles and periods. The study was my favourite room and we had most of our books in there along with the record player and two cases of model soldiers. With a coal fire burning in the beautiful grate the room came alive and reflections would dance off the pieces of copper and brassware dotted round the room. I had been lucky enough to bid for an old fashioned battered leather suite which fitted the room perfectly with its velvet seat cushions and brass upholstery tacks all around the arms. It had cost me one pound and I couldn't understand why nobody had shown any interest in it.

I had been doing my general market research for about a year when something potentially more interesting came up. It was market research again but this time *farm* research. At the interview the area manager had explained how the system worked.

'On your application form you have to confirm that you have the use of a car. You'll need it for this job – there's no way you can manage without. We issue the work in the form of map references and you have to identify which two-kilometre square of the Ordnance Survey map we are talking about. Sometimes the research area is in bigger blocks; you'll have to check your maps. You can read a map I assume? – it's essential.'

'Oh, yes,' I agreed. 'I love navigating and I always use OS maps,' I added, laying it on thick.

'Right, I'll continue. You have to be able to tell as you drive along a road or lane exactly when you are crossing the imaginary grid-line. Then, within the boundary of that square you have to investigate all the farms and smallholdings. They won't necessarily be shown on your map but you'll have to drive down each turning and track to check – until you are out of the square – that is, over the imaginary line.'

'Ye-es,' I had faltered, wondering what the assertive woman was going to tell me next.

'The size of farm we are interested in will be stated on each assignment and the questionnaire will contain sections from several different companies. You are an experienced market researcher so I won't have to explain about how to ask questions and record the answers without any bias. Do you think you would like the job?'

'Yes,' I replied quickly. 'My agricultural training would be useful I should think. I'll know what I'm talking about and I won't feel out of place on farms. Then there's my map reading skills...' I tailed off as I wondered briefly about our car.

Since my first car, an old upright black Ford Popular, had been written off after a minor prang I had been without one for several years. Then Bryn and I had bought an ancient mushroom coloured Ford Anglia. From there we had progressed through an A30 which I had painted emerald green, an A35, a Morris 1000 and an 1100. They had all been bought dirt cheap and we had run them into the ground. Now we had splashed out and were the proud owners of a second-hand Ford Anglia with the inward sloping rear window, considered an innovative design. Unlike our earlier cars which were held together under the bonnet with wire coat hangers and whose body work was repaired with flattened out baked bean cans patched on with Isopon this new car looked quite smart. I just hoped it was up to the job of bumping down farm tracks.

'We'll pay you a mileage allowance of course. What size car engine have you got? You would start off on one batch of interviews a month and you would have seven days to fit them in. We'll let you know soon and if you are successful there will be two days training,' the woman continued briskly.

That evening I relived my interview as I told Bryn everything about it.

'It's up to you I suppose,' he admitted. 'What will I do about my lunch on the days you work?'

'You could take sandwiches maybe, then I could get a meal in the evening. Or I could put a casserole in the oven on slow cook and you could serve yourself.' Luckily I had already thought about this.

'OK then, you may as well give it a go. I can see you want to,' Bryn agreed, rather reluctantly.

'I'll give up my cleaning job if I get the farm research. I'm just about brassed off with those offices. That'll mean I can be with the children at tea-time and it'll take the pressure off you. I like to be here when Dylan is doing his homework.' I hoped that would quell any misgivings he had and it wasn't many days until the postman brought a letter offering me a job.

My first assignment arrived in the post and I eagerly identified the square on the Ordnance Survey map I had been issued with. My patch was an enormous one, from the Malvern Hills in the west over to the start of the Cotswolds in the east. It went up to the borders of Birmingham and down to Cheltenham. They hadn't said so in as many words but I was covering the whole of Worcestershire. The square that I marked out in pencil looked quite insignificant and I was glad they had started me off gently.

I passed over the imaginary grid square on the country lane after navigating past junctions and under pylons. A peeling farm sign pointed down a rough track and I turned off and bumped into potholes and slewed about on loose gravel. A superb half-timbered farm house came into view flanked by a traditional farmyard and huge barn. The border collies kicked up a din and bounded over to the car as soon as I pulled up. I spoke to them as I climbed out and put my hand out for them to sniff feeling relieved when they lost interest in me and streaked after a cat. No-one came out of the buildings and there was no sound of activity anywhere so I made my way towards the back door.

'Good morning,' I began. 'I'm from Farm Research and I was hoping to speak to the farmer.'

'You'll have a job; he's out drilling the wheat. Right up in Wood Field, a long walk,' the woman pointed vaguely in the direction of a distant belt of woodland. 'Come in for a coffee, he might come back for elevenses.'

'I'd love to but I'd better carry on to my next farm,' I said reluctantly for I had looked over her shoulder at the traditional kitchen with Windsor chairs round a huge table and a cream Aga with a pan of something heating up on the hotplate. 'Could you mention that I'll try to call back later in the week? Any idea which day would be best?' I scribbled myself a reminder and walked over to the car. Slowly driving back up the rutted lane I felt disappointed that my first call had been a no-result.

A quarter of a mile down the road I didn't have to look far for the farm. The yard gate led me straight off the road and this time I could see cattle. A man with his sleeves rolled up was forking silage into a wooden manger which ran the length of the stock barn. He turned to call to me.

'The boss is over there in the office,' he nodded towards a black painted door set into the rich red brickwork then turned back to his work.

I knocked on the door and stepped inside when a voice yelled 'Yes?'

I went through my introduction and the farmer said,

'Come on then. I've got ten minutes. What to you want to know?'

I launched into my questionnaire asking about the rate of fertilizer application, the month of year applied and the brand used. Then came the section about whether he was happy with the results from the brand he used. I swiftly continued with questions about feed-stuffs, herbicides and farm implements.

'How many acres do you farm? I asked as I turned to the back page. 'Could you tell me how many head of stock you have please, then I've finished?' Relief must have been evident in my voice.

'Come over to the house for a cuppa; I could do with one,' he invited with a grin, and we trooped across the concrete yard towards the farmhouse.

Later I ate my sandwiches in the car and decided that one more farm would be enough for my first day although there were some lanes I hadn't driven down yet – they could wait for another day.

Over the next six months I called at many more farms and although some were over towards Malvern most of them fell in a rough square bounded by Redditch, Worcester, Tewkesbury and Evesham. Sometimes I had to walk along beside a tractor, bellowing the questions to make my voice heard above the roar of the engine. Sometimes I spent an hour in a delightful kitchen sharing my farming experiences with the farmer's wife. I worked in rain and sleet, sunshine and wind but at least I had the freedom to choose which days of the week to work. Our car suffered badly and over the months several bits dropped off as I was bumping down farm tracks. In the end I decided I had better call it a day even though we needed the money I earned. It seemed an irony that many of the market researchers drove huge petrol guzzling cars and looked as though they could easily manage without their hard earned pay cheque!

* * * * *

I had experienced six months without my evening cleaning job and I had grown used to being with the children from the time they arrived home after school until they went to bed. I had relaxed more into my role as a mother and I was always ready to play with them, listen to their tales about school and help with their various projects but often the time was taken up by separating the sparring brothers.

Max had been at school about a year by now and the teachers had found him rather a handful with his short attention span, inclination to be disruptive but obvious ability to grasp new facts. Luckily his teacher was able to devote some individual time to him and although he was out of kilter with the rest of the class she would set him extra work. His end-of-term reports told us what we already knew: Max could do better if he could concentrate.

Dylan meanwhile did not seem to be thriving at St Egwins Middle School. After a very promising start at Swan Lane he seemed to lose enthusiasm for study and just marked time doing only the bare essentials.

Bryn and I spent hours discussing the boys and their characters. Max still took over most of the action at home and insinuated his dominant personality over everyone and everything. There was a constant battle of wills between him and us and he seemed to take a delight in being defiant. He still disrupted anything Dylan was doing and managed to transfer the blame for any naughtiness to his brother. Inevitably Dylan would resent being the scapegoat especially when he was unfairly accused.

Bryn didn't always see Dylan's point of view and would usually give way to Max's unyielding demands and undermine my attempts at imposing discipline by striking bargains or sanctions. Not only was I at my wits end wondering how to encourage our seven year old son to behave in a reasonable way but had to make compromises because Bryn believed in a more laid back approach and would never impose any punishment. He didn't like to be tough one and it was usually me who laid down the law and suffered by being unpopular.

'Dad, can I go out on my bike for an hour before bedtime?' Max would ask, hanging on the door knob.

'Have you asked your mother? What does she say about it? Bryn would question, glancing up from the Melody Maker.

'Well, she said no; I've got to have a bath, but *please* Dad, go on, let me,' Max wheedled.

'No. You'd better not I suppose,' Bryn continued, sounding undecided.

'Go on, Dad. It won't matter.'

'Oh, go on then, you may as well,' Bryn gave in, wanting to get back to his paper.

On the rare occasions when family life was running smoothly the children could be a delight and we would have happy times watching each stage of their childhood. Max loved dressing up and would don hats, false noses and wigs as well as funny outfits and strut around acting the part. Bryn's interest in military uniforms and model soldiers rubbed off on the children and they loved Action Man and spent their pocket money on new uniforms and begged for bigger items like a sit-on armoured car as presents. Their jointed dolls would be hurled about in imaginary conflict, hung from the banisters and doused in buckets of water. Tiny kit-bags and weapons would be scattered all over the house and garden and these minuscule accessories would sometimes slip down the sides of the sofa. Both boys loved drawing and would sketch scenes of mayhem and death and embellish their pictures with lurid colours.

At weekends we would sometimes go on an expedition to a regimental museum or drive slowly past the Army vehicle depot at Ashchurch so the children could see armoured personnel carriers, landing craft and the occasional tracked vehicle. We took them to the Imperial War Museum and Bovington Tank Museum where they absorbed every aspect of a military campaign.

Bryn tried to allay my fears about encouraging aggression and a jingoistic attitude in the boys. He reminded me that he was a pacifist despite his interest in warfare, weapons and uniforms and insisted that there would be no detrimental effect on the children's personalities – if anything he said, their knowledge would make them more rounded people.

In addition to being fascinated by all things military they enjoyed the more usual pleasures of childhood including playing outside with friends, riding their bikes or making dens.

I had boundless energy, both physical and mental and was always keen to take on a new challenge or interest. After I had attended the *Women in Literature* class for ten weeks some of us had decided to form a Women's Group in Cheltenham. Often using the topics raised in *Spare Rib* as a starting point we would earnestly discuss work, health, sex, the family, politics, law and order or education, all from a women's perspective. My sociology classes had given me an extra insight and I found that I could confidently put my point of view. Several members were quite militant feminists who were prepared to put themselves on the front line for women's rights.

The core of the group – Hazel, Angela, Cathy, Pat, me and a few others thought it would be marvellous if Cheltenham had its own Women's Centre and decided to lobby the council for a property where we could meet, display literature, have a drop-in centre and even eventually open a refuge. After a month or so of prolonged pressure we were eventually offered a run down terraced property in lower High Street and with excited anticipation began to decorate and furnish it with a desk, old filing cabinets, notice boards and bookshelves. Wearing my scarlet dungarees and baseball boots I drove over to Cheltenham whenever I could but I had taken on another commitment by then.

At the top of our road where a gravelly track led off between fruit trees was an imposing 1930s detached residence. The lady of the house had advertised for someone to help with housework and I had applied. It was too good an opportunity to miss; it would only take a couple of minutes to walk there. She had outlined my duties and hoped that I could split the work into two two-hour shifts and just before nine-thirty one sunny Tuesday morning in the early summer of 1979 I had strolled up the road and turned down the drive between drifts of white plum blossom. I had walked round to the back door to begin my new job knowing how much I was going to enjoy working in this lovely house.

'Come in Angela,' Mrs Barnard had invited. 'Hang your coat in the back porch then I'll show you the cleaning materials and vacuum cleaner.'

I had brought an apron to wear but my employer passed me a nylon overall and led me into the kitchen.

'My husband spends most mornings doing his paperwork and we usually have our coffee about ten thirty. I'll come in today and show you how we like it and then you can bring it in for us. You can have one too – there's a stool for you under the kitchen table.'

I had known after only one morning that I had made the right choice and I thoroughly enjoyed working for these friendly and civilised people.

Bryn hadn't forgotten his wander-lust; for him the grass was always greener on the other side of the fence and when we visited his mother in

Torquay that summer he suggested that we might consider moving to Exeter. A couple of days wandering round the estate agent's offices in that affluent city soon changed his mind and he switched his interest to Plymouth. I had been going to Plymouth regularly now for well over twenty years and liked the feeling of it and its proximity to the sea. I reluctantly agreed to consider the idea of house-hunting thinking it wouldn't take long to work that out of Bryn's system. Surprisingly there were several houses that I found appealing, ones with that certain extra something to recommend them and I began to take seriously the idea of moving. We decided to arrange another weekend in Devon to begin to view the ever increasing list of potential properties. By the autumn we had decided on one; a double-fronted stuccoed villa off Beaumont Road and we returned to Evesham to put our house on the market.

We had always kept everything up together and the décor had been influenced by the period of the property. Our mix of furniture from the past one hundred and fifty years seemed to fit effortlessly into the house and the ambience was one of shabby chic. Our own paintings along with some reproductions hung in every room and my growing collection of bric-a-brac was offset by Bryn's books and models. We liked the house but would other people? Within a couple of weeks we had an offer of the asking price and we felt that was a good profit on our original purchase price considering we had only been there four years. Our mortgage was still extremely low; we had never been able to afford to increase it as Bryn's wages had not risen significantly. Our bigger and better houses were partly the result of accidentally buying and selling at the right time and partly, we thought, because of the way we had decorated and presented them.

With tense anticipation we set in motion the process of buying a new house but our excitement was short-lived. Someone in the chain had backed out and the deal fell through. I consoled myself by thinking of all I was involved in at Evesham. I had given up my evening cleaning job now that I went up the road twice a week, I did market- and farm-research interviewing three or four days a fortnight and my own housework filled in the rest of the weekdays. I had called a halt to the second year of my sociology course – I simply couldn't spare the time, not just to go to the classes but to complete the assignments of essays, reading and research, but I thought one day I might continue with my studies. I had wheedled my way out of designing the church poster every week and in truth my church attendance was very spasmodic now.

However I still felt very involved in the Women's Group and relied on the sisterly comradeship to keep me focused on feminist issues. We had a Reclaim the Night march to draw public awareness to the safety, or lack of it, of women walking along the streets at night and one evening we marched round town brandishing home made placards. We fought for a Women's Right to Choose, the campaign for abortion on demand and women's right to take charge of their own body. The list of feminist causes was a long one and we were spoilt for choice when deciding on a new crusade.

Meanwhile, Bryn had not given up on the idea of moving and the hunt for a house in Plymouth continued. One damp and blustery day at the end of October 1979 we decided on the spur of the moment to drive over the Tamar Bridge on the western edge of the suburbs of Plymouth and venture into Cornwall.

The countryside seemed different as we drove west. It was greener despite the approach of autumn and there were more trees, beginning to turn colour now and the drizzle collected and dripped from the ends of the sodden foliage. We drove up and down the switchback of the A38, past turnings to villages with unknown names. Liskeard lay ahead and we decided to make that our destination, eighteen miles or so from Plymouth. The town sheltered in a hollow above the by-pass and as we edged our way along the unfamiliar approach we saw that many of the buildings were squat and solid with blocks of stone evident beneath a layer of damply peeling plaster. We pulled up on the Parade and checked for parking restrictions, then spotting an estate agent, we thought we may as well have a look at what Cornwall had to offer.

An hour later and we were ready to find a café to digest our findings from the three local agents. We felt relieved that we had left Dylan and Max in the care of Bryn's mother with a promise that they would visit their two cousins Nick and Matt. The houses pictured on the sheets we had laid out next to the tea pot on the plastic tablecloth were a mixed bunch. Some were typical Cornish cottages, solidly built of local granite and some were irregular shaped small houses which had been added to over the years and were usually rendered and painted to unify the extensions. A few were rather unappealing terraced houses overshadowed by other buildings and one imagined always in perpetual shade; even in the photographs slimey green algae was evident on the exterior walls. We were used to regular Victorian terraces of brick houses with a decent ceiling height and big sash windows: if we were serious about moving to Cornwall we would have to make some compromises.

I felt ambivalent about uprooting from my home county and shifting to the far south-west. I had finally given in to Bryn's pleas to leave Evesham and thought that Plymouth might make an acceptable base. We would be near a centre of employment, near the facilities and amenities of a city and as a bonus, near the sea. I recognised Bryn's wish to live in the county of his birth, but was Cornwall a bridge too far?

It did answer one point we had discussed long and hard. We weren't happy that our children seemed to be growing up expecting to be full members of the consumer society. In Evesham they were surrounded by friends from families far more affluent than ours who asked for, and received, bigger and better gifts every year; more expensive bikes, shoes, branded clothes, even designer school bags. We told ourselves that even if we had the money the children's wishes would not be fulfilled. We despised the consumer society and the trend to make everything disposable. The word on the street was that you didn't fit in if you couldn't boast the latest wristwatch or animated video game. Our children didn't have them and sometimes they were picked on and made fun of. We talked over these points as we sat in the cafe waiting for the rain to stop. Would Cornwall hold the answer? We hoped that it might.

We had promised to be back in Torquay by teatime so we drove to three addresses that looked potentially interesting, Rosemellion Terrace, Endsleigh Terrace and Oak Park Terrace. The other properties in outlying districts would have to wait for a return visit later in the half-term week.

As the sun began to set we drove back across the River Tamar on the suspension bridge opened in 1961 and looked across to the parallel Royal Albert railway bridge designed by Isambard Kingdom Brunel, in service since 1859 and linking Devon to Saltash.

We glanced down far below to see the water flowing by riverside cottages at St Budeaux before it wound past Torpoint and Devonport on its way to Plymouth Sound and we made for Torquay at the end of a busy day.

Once the children had gone to bed we took the remaining house details out of our backpack and spread them on the table in the living room at

Bryn's Mum's flat, trying to locate the villages on the handy map from an estate agent. Menheniot, Quethiock, Pensilva, Duloe and Linkinhorne; the strange sounding names seemed to reinforce their isolation. We had decided to make Liskeard our base for house-hunting and thought that a five mile radius would be manageable, so we thinned out the pile and put the four remaining ones on one side to visit in a couple of day's time.

Before we went back to Evesham we had definitely decided against some locations but felt we hadn't enough choice to make a final decision. We asked to be placed on the mailing list with a promise to return in the New Year – houses didn't sell very quickly here, the agents told us.

From what we had seen I was not convinced we would find a nice house. I loved the feel of Cornwall and remembered our previous four holidays when we had been drawn into the strange exciting atmosphere of this magical county but my emotions had run away with me and I wanted a solid granite farmhouse under a clump of beech trees or a clap-board boat house on the beach. In more prosaic moments I realised that the reality would not match the expectations and we would probably end up with a house not dissimilar to the one we lived in already.

By now, at least, we were united in our desire to move there. I remembered the time seven years ago when we had briefly talked of joining a commune. We hadn't sought LSD or magic mushroom-induced highs and we didn't need the long hair, kaftan wearing summer of love approach; we just wanted a self-sufficient community where we could escape Tory politics, the Consumer Society and money-grabbing control freaks. Back in 1974 all we had done was to talk about it but these spiral conversations always came back to the same thing.

'We would pool our resources and our talents,' Bryn had said wistfully with a faraway look in his eyes. 'If we had the right mix of people we could cultivate the land and grow vegetables.'

'Perhaps,' I had agreed tentatively for Bryn wasn't interested in gardening. 'But we could cook and eat communally, that would be fun,' I had enthused, with a vision of a long table and me ladling out the delicious and nourishing stew I had cooked on the Rayburn.

'Who would do the washing up? You wouldn't want to if you'd cooked the meal,' Bryn had accurately prophesied. 'Would we have to have a rota with some people doing shopping and cooking, some doing laundry and some people cleaning?'

'I guess so, as long as it wasn't always the women doing the domestic stuff.' My dream had run on to a huge chart with a dozen names down the side and the week's jobs along the top with the squares neatly coloured in so you could see at a glance who was doing what.

'What do you see yourself offering?' I had enquired, wondering where Bryn's talents of letter writing, music appreciation and sketching would fit in.

'Perhaps I could write a news letter or press releases and print them up on an old Gestetner; anyway I like baking and cooking too and I could always learn some new skills.

We had sat in a rosy contemplation of this idyllic lifestyle until reality seeped in.

'Would everyone want to work every day? Would the others want to get up and start work at 7.30? Would there be any breakfast when it was their turn to cook?' We had questioned each other with a mounting suspicion that the commune residents may be looking for a laid-back lifestyle with few or no responsibilities. We began to think we were being rather naïve to hope that everyone would delight in pulling together for the common good.

I had a well defined work ethic passed down via generations of hard grafters. I enjoyed work for its own sake; I couldn't help it; it was the way I was. I had decided that commune life wouldn't be for me. I realised that I would soon grow resentful if I was the only person to do the work and the others were dossing around. Of course, it might not be like that but I had felt I couldn't take the risk.

Now, faced with the chance to move to Cornwall and have a change of scenery and lifestyle I felt more confident that we might make a go of a more self-sufficient lifestyle.

It was the end of February before we could return and we set aside a few days to try and finalise our choice of a new house. We hadn't seen a place we liked within Liskeard and we began to venture into the villages beyond. South of the town were lush valleys with jungle vegetation and glimpses of rivers and streams. We avidly read the history of these settlements, turning to the *Shell Guide to Cornwall* for John Betjeman's wordy and perceptive descriptions.

We felt the villages mouldering between Liskeard and the coast at Looe were claustrophobic with their holy wells and their secrets, so we turned north to the uplands and climbed the lanes to the open spaces of Bodmin Moor. Feeling liberated we aimed the car up the left fork off the Launceston road and followed the printed route on the estate agents details to a clutch of viewings in St Cleer and beyond. As we passed between the high banks topped with sparse stunted thorn bushes we began to feel the essence of the Cornwall described by Daphne du Maurier in *Jamaica Inn*. We drove slowly past cottages in Tremar, Darite and Crows Nest not seeing a property we wanted to view. Having driven round and out of the bungalow dominated Pensilva we felt less confident of our choices.

There was one house left and Hennings had made it sound quite interesting. Back on the Launceston road we turned left at Upton Cross and immediately began to climb a narrow lane. Through gateways we glimpsed distant views of derelict buildings with tall chimney stacks and huge heaps of stones tumbled against the granite walls. We spotted trackways winding along the contours of the hills and guessed they might be old railway lines serving the disused mine workings. After passing a few farms nestling in dells sheltering under gnarled trees we approached the outskirts of the village of Minions. An outlying cluster of solid semi-detached houses set on a bank flitted past on the right before we reached the nucleus of the village and pinpointed the house we had come to see.

The owners told us enthusiastically of its history as they led us round the unconventional layout and we took in the period details of this unusual building – not a cottage yet not quite a terraced house although it was in a terrace. Our questions were answered carefully as we sat beside the stone fireplace overshadowed by a huge copper canopy and gratefully held mugs of steaming tea.

We decided to walk round the village to see what it had to offer and as we noted the pub and the shop and the dusty white tracks leading onto the moorland Bryn and I exchanged our feelings about the house.

'Well, what do you think?' I asked, to get the ball rolling.

'I like it; it certainly has character. Pity there's not much of a garden,' Bryn responded. 'Do we like it enough to make an offer?'

'We certainly must make up our minds soon. We really wanted to have moved by the time Dylan would start a comprehensive school and it's already half way into that year. I love the openness and feeling of freedom here and the rugged sense of beauty,' I added to the debate.

'The industrial archaeology is fantastic, isn't it? Then there are all the historic sites; stone circles, tumuli, hill forts and standing stones. It seems just our sort of place,' said Bryn, summarising my own feelings. 'Shall we pop back and have another quick look?'

'OK, just to reassure ourselves but if everything is alright then let's have it!' I concluded, feeling excitement welling up inside me.

At the end of the day we called back at the estate agents and told them we would be making an offer for the house and driving back to Torquay we began to formulate our plans for a new lifestyle in this quirky house.

Chapter 7

Minions Row, Minions, Cornwall

Skylarks were manically singing high above the golden gorse on the open moorland at the end of our row as we watched anxiously for the two pantechnicons to arrive. The children were staying with Bryn's mother in Torquay for a couple of days while we got the house sorted but we couldn't do much until our furniture arrived. The drivers had over-nighted in Plymouth but should have been here by now. It was the last week of May and we had said our farewells in Evesham and at last moved to Cornwall.

We had managed to secure a mortgage by being economical with the truth. Not surprisingly the building society would not give us a mortgage unless one of us had a job so Bryn had told them he would stay in Evesham working at the printing office until he could get a job in Cornwall. This much was true: once we had moved the furniture in and brought the children down he would be lodging with some friends near our old house. How easy it would be to find a job here in Cornwall or how long he would stick it in digs remained to be seen.

The two huge furniture lorries finally arrived and the drivers were grateful that we had asked the local police to put out some hazard signs in the narrow bottle-neck formed by the end of Minions Row. Some hours later and fortified by cups of tea they headed back towards the Tamar Bridge and the M5 and we were left with randomly dumped furniture to lug into place. We had only seen the house twice before and we hadn't decided on the positions for all our assorted bits and pieces.

The rooms were fairly well defined so once the dining room was sorted out all the rest had somehow to fit in the sitting room. We were pleased with our new abode and as we heaved the sofas and bookcases into a pleasing arrangement we exchanged memories of what the previous owner had told us.

The village of Minions had been founded in the early nineteenth century by miners working the copper and tin seams across the moors and was the highest settlement in Cornwall at 300 metres. At first it was like a shanty town of rough huts called Cheesewring Village, and then granite cottages were erected as families put down roots. By all accounts the miners were a lawless and uncouth lot and evangelical Methodists moved in to try and instil morality amongst the wild and heathen hordes.

A Wesleyan chapel had been erected at the edge of the village on the road to Upton Cross and then a Bible Christian chapel was built on the end of a row of eight miners' cottages. Eventually, towards the end or the nineteenth century an extension was added and the enlarged building became a Temperance Hotel. During the 1950s these premises were divided into two and one of them, the one that had been the chapel, was our new house. It was a story that appealed to us and the previous owner had shown us the original harmonium that had been left behind and the high ceilings and long windows testified to the building's former use.

Towards the end of that half-term week we drove up to Torquay to collect the boys from their grandmother's and introduce them properly to their new home. A day at the shops got them kitted out for their new schools: Dylan was to attend Callington Comprehensive and Max would go to the local Upton Cross Junior School.

On Sunday we said goodbye to Bryn as he made the journey back to Evesham and work, while I was left to settle into the village on my own. I soon sorted out a lift to school each day and avoided trekking up the steep narrow lane with Max in tow. Dylan's school bus called at Minions just after eight o'clock each morning and he began to make a few friends on the journey.

Five weeks later we were reunited as a family; the inevitable had happened and Bryn had hated sticking it out without the rest of us and given his notice in. He was officially unemployed and next week presented himself at the Unemployment Benefit Office in Launceston to sign on. We saved petrol by combining the trip with a visit to Norman's Cash and Carry to stock up on groceries and this became the pattern for a couple of years until Bryn was allowed to declare his unemployment by post.

The summer holidays were soon on us and we delighted in walking on the moor with the children; there was so much to explore.

The first place to visit was The Hurlers, a complex of three stone circles tucked in behind our row of houses. We boned up on the history and discovered they were about three and a half thousand years old and dated from the Bronze Age. Many of the stones were fallen and lay in the coarse grass with heather growing over the rough pitted granite. Two tall sentinel stones kept guard over the linking circles from a little way off and a buried paved track cutting through the centre of the rings led to a tumulus a couple of hundred yards distant. I wondered what Celtic holy man had led processions through the stone circles to the burial site of a chief and whether the warring Dumnomi tribe had settled in this high, easily defended area.

We were thrilled to be so close to a mysterious prehistoric site but rather surprised that there wasn't an information board outlining its history or telling the legend of The Hurlers. Local people seemed to take it for granted and paid it scant attention. We were eager to wander further afield and look at other relics of ancient tribes and of industrial archaeology.

On our next walk we tried to find Minions Mound the tumulus that gave the village its later name but the surface of the moor was so pock-marked with evidence of open cast mining it was difficult to see what was what. Instead, we allowed the raging wind to blow us up the slope of the moor to a grassy mound we hoped was the barrow associated with The Hurlers. On the eastern side of the knoll was a rough, low doorway crudely fashioned from three pieces of granite. Shielding the children from the wind we all crouched down to squint inside, hoping to see evidence of ancient burials. The damp stonework glistened with an iridescent glow from algae colonising the rocks where the sun never shone. Our reference book told us it was called Rillaton Barrow and in 1837 some men digging there for building stone had unearthed a ribbed gold cup which was now displayed in the British Museum after a stint as the King's shaving mug! The top of the burial mound had caved in and a brackish pool supported clumps of rushes.

We were glad to get back home out of the wind; although it was summer a breeze blew through the village most days – it stands at a thousand feet above sea level. We soon realised that the other weather extremes were sheeting rain or low cloud that would persist for days and obliterate the television mast on Caradon Hill a mile away.

As the weeks passed we made other forays onto the moor and the most spectacular feature was the Cheesewring an immense pile of weathered granite boulders towering above the rim of a quarry. These naturally eroded rocks tottering on the edge of the Iron Age hill fort of Stowe's Pound had been a tourist attraction for a couple of centuries. Scrambling up the steep slope we spotted the rough rock-shelter of Daniel Gumb, a stone-cutter in the eighteenth century, who brought his family out to live on the moor near to where he plied his trade. According to our guide book he had an interest in mathematics and had carved Pythagoras's Theorem on the cap-stone of his rough abode. Unable to believe our eyes we traced our fingers over the squares and triangles etched in the pitted granite and imagined his wife trying to care for her husband and children in this isolated spot.

Decorating our new home was not a priority as it was papered throughout with coarse woodchip painted either white or cream but I tried to give the rooms extra character with curtains, rugs and lamps. The overwhelming style of the dining room was influenced by my collection of 1930s Art Pottery which filled the shelves in the alcove. For the curtains I had found some abstract design fabric in angular orange and yellow and the jagged shapes reinforced the bizarre patterns on the pottery. Our pine dining table and chairs filled the space perfectly leaving the dresser to fit into the other alcove. The room was fitted with a solid-fuel Parkray heater which also heated the water but as the room was used infrequently it wasn't cost effective to run the stove. In any case once we had used the supply of anthracite in the fuel bunker out in the back yard we couldn't afford to buy more. The night-storage heater would have to be enough for the fast approaching autumn.

Another heater sat in the double hall and barely took the chill off the landing and staircase. The huge stone fireplace with its chunky iron fire basket that had looked so appealing in the sitting room now looked gloomy and barren since the previous owners had taken the log cradle with them. I wasn't sure how we could burn a fire on the stone slabs or even where we would find any wood. For now, as in the dining room, the big old-fashioned night storage heater would have to do this winter. The wind rattled the wooden sash windows and I thought we would be slotting folded newspapers into the gaps in another couple of months. Until then I wanted to let light flood into the room and we maximised it with cheap slatted roller blinds that could be pulled right up to the top of the frame. Glints of copper and brass gave some warmth and our pieces of antique furniture added solidity to the room.

We were already feeling the pinch; the dole wasn't much, even the combined unemployment and supplementary benefit and we had a mortgage to pay as well as having a bigger house to run. One of us would have to get a job and we both searched the situations vacant columns of the Cornish Times. There were a few printing jobs but too far away to consider seriously: Plymouth, St Austell, Truro, Bodmin; we doubted whether our car would hold up to that sort of regular driving. We had invested our last bit of spare cash in a Hillman Avenger, but truth to tell it was on its last legs; it was advertised as being suitable to break up for spares but we thought we could get another couple of thousand miles out of it before it finally clapped out.

A local day-centre for adults with special needs was asking for an escort to accompany one of the mini-bus drivers on his rounds, collecting the clients from their homes and returning them in the afternoon. The thing that caught my eye was that the journey started from Upton Cross, the nearest village to us. I thought I would ask for an application form and find out a few more details. An interview followed in ten days time and I was offered the job. The hours were going to be difficult; I was needed at just the time I would be getting Dylan and Max off to school and again when I liked to be around to welcome them back and make them a drink. Bryn and I had talked it over and he was willing to take over my role at these two times and in any case, he hadn't anything else to do. At the beginning of the autumn term I presented myself at seven-thirty on a damp morning down by the cross roads to meet Harold the van driver.

The route was beautiful and over the next few weeks I got to know it like the back of my hand: we would head out to Bray Shop then Kelly Bray, turning left along the northern side of Kit Hill, the eye-catching mound crowned by a chimney stack, near Callington where the trees were beginning to change colour. Downgate, Monkscross, St Ann's Chapel, picking up along the way, then down into Gunnislake for a couple of other passengers. More stops at ancient houses in the steep hidden valleys leading down to the mighty Tamar River then when we had our full quota of a dozen passengers we headed back to Liskeard and the Morley Tamblyn Day Centre on Lodge Hill. Once I had escorted everyone into the centre Harold would waste no time in getting us back to base and I drove back up to Minions to sit on the storage heater in the lounge and warm myself up with a cup of tea and a slice of toast.

After two or three weeks both Bryn and I had settled into our new roles. He would make sure the boys got up on time, give them breakfast and check they had everything ready for school. Once Dylan had caught the bus it was time to organise Max ready for his lift – or sometimes to walk him down to school. By the time I got home the washing up was done and the kitchen tidied up.

Meanwhile I was getting to know the people in the mini-bus. They had a variety of disabilities, some Downs Syndrome, some Cerebral Palsy and some epilepsy. Others, I wasn't so sure about but without fail they were always ready for the transport and came out of their front doors smiling with anticipation at the day ahead. I grew fond of them all and learnt their idiosyncrasies and they began to trust me and show affection. Over the months I discovered some of the subjects the centre offered. Gardening, craftwork, pottery and keep-fit were amongst the favourite activities for my bunch and for those who were able there were academic lessons. The atmosphere was stimulating yet calm; bright paintings, banners and sculptures adorned the entrance foyer as everyone moved purposefully about the contemporary building. I enjoyed my job and looked on myself as a tiny cog in the well-oiled machinery of running the centre.

My pay made only a slight difference to our standard of living because of course for every pound I earned our benefit was reduced by a pound. The eighteen hours a week I worked meant that we had a little more in the housekeeping purse but we needed extra income from somewhere. The winter would soon be upon us, our job search would have to wait until spring; unless something turned up for Bryn it would be time to consolidate what progress we had made in our first six months.

Along the back of the houses ran a wide track giving access to the garages and separating the gardens from the houses. Our house just had a back yard where the fuel bunker sat and the washing line flapped about strung on its pulley. Across the track and slightly offset was our big garage where we stored the redundant lawnmower, the children's bikes, our garden tools and a few odds and ends for the car. We stowed everything neatly and swept out the dust and cobwebs. I had finished with the tools until spring after forking over our front garden and resetting some heavy stones along the edge of the path. I'd cadged some plants from Mum's patch and rearranged the few perennials that were there and hoped it would make a colourful show next year. The

Angie outside Runwell House, May 1980.

brown crock sink that we had brought down from Evesham was positioned to the left of the door with some new rockery plants trailing over the pebbles I had set in the sandy soil. As I crouched low, scratching at the soil I looked forward to the time when May Holman would stop for a chat as she encouraged her cows up the road to outlying fields along the moor. Actually, there wasn't much to do outside and I was already longing for a place to dig.

Liskeard was our nearest town and we called there every week to do our top-up shopping and to visit the market hall and library. We gravitated to a café in Lower Lux Street called The Rainbow for a cuppa and slice of carrot cake and soon began to recognise faces and add a few names. The atmosphere was lively and they displayed many posters on the community notice board. As we perused these we noticed that people were offering a whole range of services from gardening to decorating and from craftwork to yoga. The café seemed the hub of alternative lifestyle interests and we soon felt at home there. Upstairs there was a craft market one day a week and Bryn and I decided to select some of our work and book a stall.

On Friday of the following week I had everything ready to pack into the car as soon as I returned from work and we arrived at the café as it opened and drew the car in to the kerb of the narrow hill. I unloaded a big black bag, a cardboard box and a pile of Bryn's paintings and started to cart them upstairs while Bryn went to park the car. I soon had an Indian throw spread on the table and some watercolour paintings ledged along the back of the stall. By the time Bryn was back I had covered most of the surface with my bright knitted and crocheted cushions adding a pile of Fair Isle berets to the side. For good measure I had included a couple of pieces of pottery that I had made in Evesham then had time to stand back and survey the other stalls. Their offerings were similar to mine: ceramics, scarves, paintings, jewellery and wooden carvings. There was a stirring on the stairs and the first customers began to trickle in. I can't say trade was brisk but I sold a couple of things and most importantly of all I loved the atmosphere and the bustle and banter. I had interesting conversations with several women and looked forward to returning the following week.

Bryn was in his element too; he had missed company and as ever had many fascinating topics to discuss, so given half a chance he would launch straight into politics, art or jazz and soon made friends with an artist called Duncan.

Over the winter months I enlarged my range of craft items on offer; I had plenty of time and had a go at making anything that took my fancy. For very little outlay I bought beads and hooks to make earrings or I bent lengths of copper electrical wire into zigzags and corkscrews to form more exotic designs. I used my, as yet untouched, box loom to weave wool landscape designs of the moors and then attach pieces of slate, wood and feathers to the knotted warp threads and suspend the hangings from lengths of drift wood. With a careful price structure I could sell several items a week and put the cash towards things we were desperate for – even if it was a magazine or a cup of coffee.

* * * * *

By the time we had been in Cornwall a year we were feeling part of the local community. The children were settled in their schools and had made friends. They still didn't get on well together and I was relieved that they had separate interests and activities. Even so Max would still take an apparent delight in being disruptive and had a well-tuned knack of getting his brother into trouble. Bryn, as a full time parent now, seemed oblivious of the need to apportion blame fairly and inevitably it was Dylan who got the sharp end of his tongue or a clip round the ear.

Max was finding school more of a challenge now that he was in a smaller class and had a teacher who could devote more time to him. Mr Wonnacott realised Max's potential to excel at maths and set him more and more advanced work and strangely Max thrived on it and didn't resent being pushed harder than many of his contemporaries. The other subject he couldn't get enough of was art. He had developed a talent for detailed pencil drawings and would be absorbed for hours with a fantasy landscape and alien creatures, completely filling the page with action-packed scenes of murder, mayhem and mystery. At home he would go off over the moor on his grifter bike with his friends Oliver and Andrew, skidding about on the slippery heather and bouncing off boulders. Sometimes I knew they had climbed on abandoned mine buildings but I realised that this derring-do was just part of growing up. They would come home with a jam jar full of leeches from Witheybrook Pool or a grass snake in their pocket.

Dylan didn't seem to enjoy school and jogged along just about scraping through except in English and Art. He enjoyed graphic design and used vibrant poster paint to make posters for all his favourite rock bands and replicated in Gothic script the logos from the leading groups. His interest in Heavy Metal music had been fuelled by his cousin Nick and he was a mine of information about musicians, band line-ups and the background stories to the big names. He took *Kerrang* magazine now he had outgrown comics and absorbed all the latest from bands such as Motorhead, AC/DC, Kiss, and the rest. He and his friend Jason played their records at top volume whilst frantically head-banging along to the pulsing drum beat and bass guitar riffs. We had bought him a denim jacket and I showed him how to sew on the coloured patches representing his favourite bands. Soon he wanted to customise his jacket and drew designs all over the back. Seeing my embroidery silks one day he asked if he could stitch round one of the designs in bright red and yellow. After learning a few basic stitches he became adept at sewing flamboyant individual designs and would earn himself extra money by customising his friends' jackets.

It wasn't just our sons who were making new friends and developing new interests. I had often been in conversation with several of the women who frequented The Rainbow and it was with pleasure and excitement that I read a poster on the notice board suggesting that women formed a Consciousness Raising Group similar to the one I had belonged to in Cheltenham. At first we met at the café but once we had built up trust we would meet at a pub or in each others homes. We discussed all the relevant women's issues of the day and gradually began confiding our hopes and fears then our aspirations and disappointments. Sometimes we would externalise these feelings to the group at large, sometimes to another woman we had developed a trusting relationship with. Over the winter we formalised ourselves as The Liskeard Women's Group. I reassessed my opinions about housework, motherhood, friendship, relationships, sex and politics – then reassessed them again. I was in a state of flux. New ideas were jostling about in my head and I was particularly rethinking my views on marriage. I felt lucky to know a family that had become famous due to their unconventional family set up. John was referred to in the press as 'Superdad – the man with two wives'; I visited both the houses of his two partners and was always given a warm welcome. By spring all my new friendships had developed and I sometimes preferred to spend time with them rather than with Bryn.

On May 19th, my thirty-seventh birthday, I opened my presents from the family; long black and gold earrings from Bryn, an Egyptian-inspired brooch from Dylan and two red notebooks from Max. The weather was thick fog, cold with a heavy dew but had started to clear by nine-thirty when I set out for Bolventor to spend the day with a new friend, Sarah. The old dilapidated farmhouse where she lived was in a sheltered position tucked into the side of a hill under a clump of beech trees and looked across towards the famous Jamaica Inn. I made friends with her two young sons before we walked along the lane as far as the ancient Codda farmstead then it was time to turn back for our lunch. Later that afternoon I drove home with my basket full of goodies: a root of borage, a brown loaf, some spinach for Dylan's rabbit Bugsie and hidden in the bottom a birthday card and pottery jug – made by Sarah. Back at home Bryn had iced and filled a coffee sponge for tea and gave me another present, one of his paintings of a dandelion in a simple pine frame.

Two days later I set up my stall once again at the Rainbow Market; full house today with the quota of six stallholders including one new person, Bryony the horse-dealer who we had often seen scuttling round the lanes with a petrol-can in her hand. It was a surprise to learn she had been to Seale-

Hayne Agricultural College just four years before me. After the first flood of customers, things dried up and my grand profit was £1.30!

My circle of friends had enlarged to include Margaret, Sheila, Claire, Diane and Jane. Fran, Annette and Cathy joined the group and we planned an event at Elephant Fair soon to be held at Port Eliot, St Germans. Our group often couldn't agree – we had some radical feminists as members and sometimes the less politically motivated women felt that their voices weren't being heard.

That summer I was invited to the home of a woman who became a life long friend. Sheila lived in an isolated cottage in the south eastern corner of the county and she had drawn a rough sketch map of how to find the house. As Bryn and I drove nearer there was a noticeable change in the vegetation; the banks and verges were wild with growth and we could see sweeping fields of lush grass and rippling barley. Her cosy and unpretentious cottage appealed to me as we passed through the scullery to the kitchen-diner and felt the warmth from the solid fuel stove. In the stone hearth of the comfortable sitting room a wood fire flamed and Sheila told us it was a very convenient house to warm. She scavenges for wood in the hedges and fields of the farm where she works and finds enough to stoke the Rayburn as well as the fire. The idea of cooking on a solid fuel stove really appealed to me but I knew it would be out of the question if fuel had to be bought. There was no wood to be picked up in Minions except sodden furze branches and Furnicite or Coalite was simply too expensive.

Over a cup of tea Sheila told us she tries to live by her ideals of anti-consumerism with as few gadgets as possible and by cutting down her outgoings. She buys her wholefood provisions in bulk from a food co-operative and rarely buys clothes. I silently mulled over these facts and although I admired this way of life and would like to adopt it myself I felt that perhaps we had been exposed to consumerism and materialism for too long. Sheila has never lived outside Cornwall and appears unexposed to city life with tempting shops and new fashions: could I cope like this I wondered. If I could get to an occasional jumble sale I might just manage but the thought of living without my washing machine – my favourite labour-saving device – well, no, I didn't think I could.

After a walk between pollen-laden hedges along the lane we tucked into a marvellous tea of home made lentil soup and brown bread followed by cheese flan, tomatoes and boiled eggs and salad. I admired my new friend's skills and ethos which she served with a liberal slice of common sense and she became a role model for the type of life I would like to live. Before we left for home she lent me a book called *Gaining Ground* by a Canadian feminist author, Joan Barfoot, and as I read the story of a woman rejecting domestic ritual and moving to a cabin to lead a secluded life whilst contemplating the position of women in society I felt an empathy with her; this book influenced me for many years. I had more time to read now and had absorbed Margaret Atwood, Anais Nin, Virginia Woolf and Margaret Drabble. These books helped to crystallize my feelings about the stage I had reached in my life and to show me other ways of doing things. *Fear of Flying* by Erica Jong and *The Awakening* by Kate Chopin were particularly influential but I also loved the revealing novels of Mary Webb and Doris Lessing's *Golden Notebook*.

In the autumn a group of us drove up to Greenham Common Women's Peace Camp which had been formed in 1981 to draw attention to the American cruise missiles that were stored on the air base. Our group were some of the thirty thousand women who held hands in a continuous chain round the base to show solidarity for the campaign to have the missiles and silos removed. We took blankets, toiletries and food for the protesters who lived in benders on the perimeter of the site and many of us wished we were able to join them. The hairs on the back of my neck stood up and my eyes filled with tears of emotion as we sang freedom songs and the classic feminist anthems.

After coping with my escort's job for a year I decided to give it up. I found the split shifts were too disruptive especially if we wanted to make an early start for a day out. However, Harold the mini-bus driver had roped me in to play badminton at Upton Cross village hall one evening a week. I hadn't played for decades but soon got into the swing of the game and really enjoyed the hard physical exercise. Whilst I was sitting a game out I would get into conversation with other villagers and together we built up a network of shared interests. I was soon co-opted onto the village hall committee whose chief job it was to run the annual Carnival and Field Day the last week in July. As the year progressed we would all be allocated individual tasks and responsibilities for this major event.

Bryn still hadn't secured a job; in fact he didn't really seem to be trying. If anything presented itself there was always a reason why it couldn't be followed up.

'Why don't you have a go at this one in Bodmin?' I would query.

'No, well, I don't feel confident with litho despite my course,' he replied, absorbed more in writing a letter to a friend than trawling through the situations vacant.

'Here's one – Plymouth though.'

'A bit far to go isn't it? Twenty five miles each way; the car won't last,' Bryn answered quickly.

'Launceston then? We've passed this place.'

'Yes, and I've looked in the door. It's just as bad as what I've left behind. I just can't do it.'

I let the subject fizzle out knowing that he would snap at me if I pushed it. We had both had to make adjustments to being together all day long but I was more used to socialising with a group of women friends and to the give and take of conversation and the exchanging of ideas. With the lack of contact with his close friends I felt Bryn was becoming dogmatic in his views and once he had the floor he would keep the subject with him, expounding his opinions and reinforcing his theories. For years I had defended him against my family but suddenly I began to understand what they meant. I knew I would need tact to sort this out; if Bryn and I were going to continue spending virtually twenty-four hours a day in each other's company we had to maintain a good relationship.

We loved walking together and our shared interest in industrial archaeology meant that when we returned from long rambles across the moors we would reach for our favourite books to consolidate the evidence we had seen on site.

A web of train lines and dram-ways connected quarries and mines with canals and railways near Liskeard and we walked out across the moor searching in the heather and bracken for half buried granite sleepers which provided evidence of a track bed. We followed the tracks past ruined engine houses and into quarries and walked on to the serrated ridge of Hawk's Tor or sometimes to the more distant Kilmar and stood with our backs to the wind scanning the horizon for a glimpse of the sea on the north Cornwall coast. To the south St Austell bay was clear and we could see the coast line as the cliffs dropped to Par. The views were certainly spectacular with the boulder strewn moorland in the foreground, the blue-green haze of fields and woods in the middle distance and the azure of the sea where it joined the pale turquoise of the milky sky. We noticed Minions was cunningly hidden in a dip and we could only spot the chimney pots above the lumps and bumps of mine workings.

Despite paying lip-service to the good life and our denial of the consumer society the highlight of Bryn's week was if we drove into Plymouth for the day. He would make tracks for Peter Russell's Hot Record Stall and take up his accustomed position ready to thumb through the albums in the racks. Better still were our frequent visits to Torquay to visit his mother which always included getting together with Kevin, Ron or John. He would take himself off to his friends' houses and immerse himself for hours on end in pure jazz and all the discussion that went with it. I stayed with Bryn's Mum swapping the latest exploits of our sons for humorous stories about her other grandsons, Nick and Matt.

I knew Bryn needed this sort of stimulating conversation and absorption in his favourite music: he always had done, what was new? It was when I pondered on all I had given up in Evesham to make our dream of isolated country living come true that I began to feel resentful. OK, the decision had been half mine; at least, I had gone along with it; but the dissatisfaction with our previous lifestyle had been all Bryn's. What was going to happen to us? I could see cracks beginning to appear.

Back in Minions we made plans to allocate individual areas of responsibility for domestic chores. Bryn loved cooking especially baking cakes and he was good at it. He had a sweet tooth and loved cakes and buns and somehow had developed the right touch. We joined the Food Co-op that operated from the Rainbow Café to buy whole foods in bulk to save cost. Each month the group would meet to place their orders; if we only wanted small quantities of anything we would ask a couple of other members if they would make up a bulk purchase. We had to reach the target order of £50 value to take advantage of the bulk-buy principle, and sometimes we ordered goods to experiment with, that we hadn't tasted before.

The co-op members would take it in turn to accept the deliveries from the lorry driver and their kitchens would become a grocery shop in miniature.

'Set the scales up level on the table,' Margaret would instruct.

'Have you got all the bags ready? The labels too?' I asked.

'They're here with a couple of pens,' Liz would chime in as we consulted a copy of our order and lined the bulk bags up on the table and floor.

The flour was the easiest to deal with as everyone, including me, ordered their flour by the sack; sometimes wholemeal, sometimes strong white. The rice was next and we cut the large paper bags open and started to ladle out Patna rice or fragrant wild rice into the brass scale pan. Once the weights were checked it was tipped into the cellophane packets and labelled up ready to go into the shopping bag of each member. Steadily we worked weighing and bagging lentils, split peas, red kidney beans and mung beans to sprout.

'Let's stop for a cuppa before we get on to the small stuff,' Margaret suggested, reaching for the kettle. 'All this dust coming off the dry goods has made me parched.'

We settled on the chairs round the kitchen table hard up against the scented geranium and had ten minutes relaxation before opening bags of fragrant spices to allocate.

The small room was redolent of an eastern bazaar as the pungent smells of ginger and curry, cinnamon and pepper or nutmeg and garam masala were released into the warm atmosphere.

Finally the end was in sight and the foil wrapped pack of yeast was lifted from the fridge to be cut up into two ounce blocks.

'I'll wipe the table down and put the scoops and scales in the sink,' I would suggest once we had finished.

'Do you need some help carrying all the shopping bags into the hall?' asked Liz.

Margaret responded with a cheerful 'No, I'll manage when you've all gone. Thanks for your help, I'll ring everyone tonight and ask them to come and collect their orders.'

With both flour and yeast in quantity Bryn decided to try some of the dough recipes from my McDougall's book. Each week he would bake a batch of buns for Sunday tea adding more delicious cakes to his repertoire – currant buns and Chelseas, doughnuts and Yorkshire tea cakes joined biscuits and sponges. He had a light touch and decided to enter some scones in a class at the Linkinhorne parish show and was delighted to receive third prize.

In the summer I would sometimes accompany Bryn on his sketching expeditions as he loped across the grass with his easy stride. He would perch on a rock and reach into his rucksack for pencils and pad. He was able to capture the essence of the moor whether it was a loosely painted landscape or a detailed scene of standing stones or maybe cotton grass round a stagnant pool.

* * * * *

In the autumn of 1981 I decided to start a new evening class. I was missing the stimulation of an academic subject and after reading through the adult education brochure I enrolled in a ten week course, *Introduction to Psychology*. I was fascinated by the topics but felt disappointed that it was so quantitative in its approach; I wanted to know the *reasons* for actions and behaviour. An old book of Dad's published as part of The Thinker's Library and called *Psychology for every man (and woman)* gave me some of the answers and padded out my course notes. During the short course we studied personality, perception, memory and group behaviour; we discovered the role of psychology in learning, moral development, role reinforcement and intelligence tests. After this I needed a break and in the spring I signed on for a course of a completely different kind.

The Landscape of Bodmin Moor was a mixture of classroom based lectures and field-work and it extended my knowledge of the moor with graphic talks on the geological, pre-historical and industrial landscape of the whole of Bodmin Moor. Some days we drove out in a hired minibus to stone circles and standing stones, tumuli and tors. The course was a combination of E C Axford's book *Bodmin Moor* and Daphne du Maurier's *Vanishing Cornwall*, and I loved every minute of it.

Once I had completed the field trips I showed Bryn the sites and we went to see the nearest places of interest. Sometimes, if money allowed and we were able to afford a couple of gallons of petrol, the whole family drove further afield. Truro and St Austell were a magnet for the occasional record shop and a decent range of magazines but usually if we went down country it would be to the coast. The quaint harbour at Charlestown has the aura of an eighteenth century village with its docks and granite quays. It was originally built for the export of china clay, mined nearby and also to ship local copper and tin. It is still possible to imagine pilchards curing in the quayside sheds and the nets hanging to dry alongside boat building yards where the tap of a mallet might sound and the sea breeze would carry the smells of fish, wood, tar and clay. We would park the car at the top of the village and wander down the street past solid granite houses until the harbour opened up and we had a view of a delightful Georgian terrace perched above the quay.

Sometimes we drove to the north coast for a trip to Tintagel or Padstow where we milled about with hundreds of tourists or explored the enigmatic

Rocky Valley where a treacherous narrow path led past ruined buildings and we passed ancient mystical labyrinths carved in the rocks as we scrambled alongside a gulley until the turbulent brook shot into the sea. Usually we made do with a trip to gentle Looe, about twelve miles away. This picturesque seaside town with its tightly packed fishermen's houses crammed round the harbour, its charming riverside frontage where the shops straggled down to the quay and its sandy beach and delightful banjo pier would keep us occupied for a whole day. We would watch the noisy gulls wheel in the seaside sky then dive down for a discarded sandwich crust or cold chip as we stomped down to the foaming wavelets or meandered along the tidemark of flotsam and jetsam until it was time to wind back along the steep overgrown valley of the East Looe River to Liskeard then on up to the wild spaces of Caradon Moor where the sun was setting behind the tors.

We had been glad to see the back of winter, our second one in our new home. It had been a bad one, the worst since 1962/3. For a start we couldn't keep warm, in fact we couldn't *get* warm. All three of our night-storage-heaters were turned up full and the paraffin stove burnt non-stop in the kitchen. We put hot water bottles in the children's beds well before bed time, and then renewed them, wrapped in a towel so the children wouldn't be burnt. Our electric under-blanket was getting rather old; we'd had it for a wedding present, but we switched it on each evening as the nine o'clock news was starting.

We badly needed something to burn in our vast fireplace but we could rarely afford a load of wood. There were very few trees on the moors, just the occasional gnarled old hawthorn, bent double in the wind. Each morning I walked round the village searching for some wood and sometimes returned with a pile of dead roots from a furze bush uprooted by the sheep. I would tie the pathetic bundle with a piece of bailer twine and sling it over my shoulder and once I was home would try to persuade it to ignite from a blazing wigwam of old vegetable crates scrounged from the shop.

Icy winds would howl around Minions Row and moorland sheep and ponies would come and shelter in the lea of our wall. We could see the snow showers approaching across the gale-whipped heather and gorse as the smoke blew down the chimney and the window frames rattled.

Some days hail stones would pound the glass and pile up inches deep on the sill. Once the snow started to fall it kept coming, first six inches then another couple the following day. Low temperatures froze it solid and after a while the children didn't even want to go out to sledge or build snowmen as shower after shower raised the level of the snow banks. There was sharp crystalline frozen rain, big soft flakes of snow and sleet sheeting over at an angle. After a few days the village was cut off and the school bus couldn't get through. We made a track over to the village shop for essential supplies and people lived off the stocks in their larders until the snow plough trundled its way up the steep hill and liberated the village. Before it did we had a day without electricity and we cooked on the Parkray stove.

That night we saw the children up to bed with a candle for light and settled them as best we could in their chilly rooms and cold beds. We were woken in the night when Dylan came in to tell us that his bed was wet.

'Something seems to be dripping, Mum,' he complained.

'Light the candle, we'd better investigate,' Bryn said, and we trooped along the landing to illuminate Dylan's wet bed. Looking up we saw water running down the cable and dripping from the light bulb to be soaked up on the duvet.

'Oh, no!' I exclaimed, 'There must be snow in the loft and it's thawing. We'll have to do something about it before it starts to come through elsewhere.'

'I'll go down for the step ladder and bring another candle up,' suggested Bryn. 'We'll have to open the loft hatch.'

Five minutes later he was on the top rung, pushing back the square of wood. With his head and shoulders through the opening his muffled voice called down to us.

'You'll never believe it! There's three inches of snow up here in places where it's blown under the slates. Somehow we'll have to clear it out.'

We put Dylan in our bed and went downstairs for buckets, washing-up bowls, dustpan and scoops. Bryn stood in the loft scraping up the snow mixed with insulating felt and passed the buckets down to me. Some of the sodden mess I emptied into the bath and some I struggled downstairs with to dump outside the door. Eventually most of it was cleared and the risk of melt-water dripping through the ceiling was averted. We squeezed into bed each side of Dylan to try and get a couple of hours sleep before Max woke for his breakfast.

Yet despite the inconvenience of that hard winter there was an elemental thrill in surviving, a feeling that we were pitching ourselves against nature. We had never really been up against it before and despite never having much money we had led rather sheltered lives and I rather enjoyed the feeling of toughing it out physically and financially.

I had expanded my second-hand dealing and taken on a weekly stall at the Butter Market in Launceston. The cold and gloomy hall with its uncompromising stone walls was divided up into stalls and I did what I could to make mine appealing. I had increased my stock by going to auction sales and house clearances across the eastern half of the county and was beginning to develop an eye for the cheaper end of the market where collectables might be bought for pence and sold for pounds. Nothing much; just ceramics and brassware, a few rugs and curtains, a picture or two and a smattering of eclectic ornaments. I liked to present my stall as if it was the sitting room or kitchen of an English country house and I draped vintage fabrics across a pine table and perched a vase of fresh flowers next to an oil lamp or stuck my aspidistra on a pine plant stand in the middle of a faded rug. It seemed to work and I slowly built up a core of people who returned each week to see what was new. As usual I couldn't resist creaming off the best of my stock for my own collection and loved blue and white striped Cornish Ware crockery and enamel storage jars.

My stall at the Rainbow Market was increasing too. I was making more jewellery and had started decorating small objects with decoupage. I had experimented with paint effects on pieces of furniture as the distressed shabby chic look began to evolve. I had been trying to think of something new to do with the driftwood I had picked up on my beach rambles and one day I had a brainwave.

I sorted out all the flat bits like old worn scraps of crates and fragments of planks, some with paint giving a patina of age and some with lettering stamped into the surface. I raided my box of magazine cuttings for pictures of old master paintings or iconic pre-Raphaelite women and cut round the images and glued them onto the drift wood. I sanded the edges of the pictures to give a worn frayed look and covered it all with a coat of yacht varnish. The finished result looked like something that had been washed up by the tide after years of being exposed to sea water. Providing I didn't try to pass off these artistic fragments as antiques I could see no harm in charging a few pounds for them. I wrote labels in spidery handwriting saying the name of the beach the driftwood had been collected from and they were surprisingly popular amongst the summer tourists.

Meanwhile my relationship with Bryn was becoming strained as we spent more time involved in separate activities. Once his chores were done he would sling his rucksack over his shoulder and stride off across the moor to paint the local scenery. He became more insular and more dogmatic. I knew he cared for me: he told me so; in fact I felt that his love for me was out of proportion, it made me feel claustrophobic, it was too much of a responsibility. I could feel us drifting apart and didn't know what to do to stop it. I felt he should be making some effort to find work; this inertia wasn't part of the plan – at least, he'd never discussed in so many words the idea of dropping out. I began to lose respect for him and the facets of his character that had originally attracted me I began to find irritating.

I had to retain some control on my life and not give up the work ethic that had always dominated my *raison d'etre*. While Bryn was bemoaning his inability to find work I advertised my services as a Jill of all Trades. I wrote out postcards offering to do cleaning, gardening or decorating for a very reasonable price and put them in local shops. Within days I had replies and these became the core of my client list whilst I fitted in casual jobs as time allowed.

Two mornings a week I cleaned a house at Rilla Mill and also did seasonal cleaning nearby when a family's weekend residence was occupied. I decorated several holiday cottages, doing all the walls in wood-chip then giving them a coat of magnolia emulsion once the woodwork was smartened up with white gloss. A local resident asked me to emulsion their sitting room and suddenly I was getting known.

On Mondays I worked in a delightful large garden with the River Lynher burbling its way through the grass edged with meadow sweet, gunnera and ladies smock and sometimes a kingfisher darted into the reeds. There was always plenty of work here to get my teeth into and I enjoyed planning the seasonal jobs.

Just up the road was the village pub and on another morning I would start by watering the window boxes and hanging baskets I had planted, then mow the grass, sweep the forecourt and weed the pretty flower beds. This job lasted all summer and I relished the feeling that I had my part in making this historic pub look attractive.

Other more varied work started to come in and I was delighted when a neighbour asked if I could take over feeding some calves and strawing-down while she had a regular morning off. It was years since I had been involved in hands-on farming and I loved the soft contact of the calves as they jostled for a slurp in a bucket of milk. The new born calves had to be trained to drink from a bucket once they had been separated from their mothers and I would dip my fingers in the warm milk and offer them to the calves to suck. Carefully I lowered my hand into the bucket so the calf's nose was submerged and they would continue to suck, finally realising they were drinking the milk without the surrogate teats. On occasions I helped to hand milk a herd of goats and I needed to relearn the skill unused by me for twenty years.

Eventually, in the autumn, I gave up my stall at the Rainbow Market. It became unviable to load the car, set up the stall, sit there for two hours then cart most of it back home just for three or four pounds – not to speak of acquiring stock or making craft items. Steady paid work took over this weekly slot but I continued at Launceston for a while longer as the tourists exploring the town and castle made up the majority of my customers.

Shortly after moving to Cornwall I became involved in three aspects of the community. I had been voted onto the Parish Hall Committee and in the spring the meetings changed pace and moved up a gear. We laid aside our more mundane agenda of hall bookings, maintenance work and jumble sales to discuss the event of the year: the Carnival.

Carnival week took place the last week of July and involved all the villages and hamlets that formed the parish of Linkinhorne. As the date loomed on my calendar hanging on a nail in the kitchen I did a mental check-list of the events I was involved in; the white elephant stall, the pet show and stewarding the procession.

The week's programme always began with the Field Day on the field at Upton Cross where the Carnival Queen was crowned. There was a sports event with classes for children and adults, food-stalls to arrange, side shows like kill-the-rat and hoopla and throwing ping-pong balls into bowls, and the White Elephant stall. I made posters and encouraged people to clear out all their unwanted gifts, their unloved ornaments and their dust-collecting bric-a-brac. Other committee members organised crockery smashing competitions, and throwing a wet sponge at a face peeping through a painted board.

I had suggested having a mid-week Pet Show and a long list of classes was arranged to include every pet in the parish. As the date got closer I booked a local vet to judge the pets and began feverishly making rosettes out of satin ribbon. Too soon the date was on us and Carnival Week began with a swing as villagers turned out for the traditional start to the week and the sun beamed down on the field where the brightly coloured bunting fluttered in a light breeze.

Skittles matches, rounders, bingo and a whist drive all followed as the week progressed. At the Pet Show the field was a cacophony of barks, yelps and yowels as children struggled up with their rabbits and hamsters, their cats and dogs and their budgies and white mice.

The event concluded with novelty classes for the cat with the longest whiskers, the dog with the waggiest tail and the pet most like its owner; by then pets and owners were flagging a little and irritability had begun to take over as the winners paraded their animals round the ring, resplendent with their rosettes and people started making tracks for home.

Carnival day at the end of the week meant a wonderful parade of floats with each local organisation decorating a lorry on which to enact a colourful tableau. Sewing machines would have been going full tilt for weeks to provide the elaborate costumes and floats from other areas would sometimes join in. A band would head the procession as it made its way slowly along the route giving ample time for the onlookers to slip coins into the collecting tins for that year's charity or wing their loose change into the buckets on the lorries. The day would end with the final ceremony and the committee were usually able to rest on their laurels having, with the active participation and support of the people of the parish, presented yet another magnificent gala.

My political energies went into the Liskeard branch of the Labour Party where I was membership secretary. Apart from canvassing for our candidate at the local elections and counting the numbers of voters at the polling booths we facilitated various other events such as a Nuclear Forum and a CND march in Callington – we had an affiliated Peace Group to carry forward the values of non-violence and non-proliferation of arms. Sometimes we rounded up our members and hired a coach to go to see a speaker such as Tony Benn or Michael Foot or to a rally or on a March for Jobs and we all felt inspired to work for a socialist future.

Seemingly at the other end of the spectrum was my involvement with the local Methodist Chapel where I helped out as a teacher for the oldest Sunday School group and all that meant; church attendance, teacher's meetings and anniversaries.

I felt firmly rooted in Cornwall and enjoyed having such diverse interests so it came as a shock to me when one day just before we had celebrated our third year in Minions, Bryn opened a conversation when the boys had gone to school.

'I don't think we can go on living here for much longer; it's simply not working.'

I was dumbfounded because for me it *was* working, and very well.

'We haven't had any money since we've been here and it looks as though I will never get any work,' he continued.

'I didn't think you'd been looking seriously,' I responded, thinking of the times I'd suggested a determined job hunt.

'If there are any jobs they go to the locals, it's a closed shop. I just can't break into it,' Bryn put in quickly. 'And there never will be any work as long as we live here.'

'Couldn't you make a last attempt,' I pleaded. 'It was you who wanted to move away from Evesham; I only agreed to please you because you seemed so unhappy.'

'OK, that's right, say it's my fault! Don't forget you were keen on the idea of self-sufficiency and look where that got us.'

He was talking about the plot of land at the top of three cottage gardens. Years ago someone wanted to build on it but it had lain unused and uncultivated for a decade or more, planning permission refused. I had traced the owner who said they wanted two hundred pounds for it so I had saved my money for almost a year and bought the land. I had spent the previous summer trying to clear a patch to grow vegetables and after weeks of digging up brambles, bracken and Rose Bay Willow herb I finally had a tiny plot to fence off and sow. Despite me making a new gate to replace the knobbly iron bedstead that had blocked the entrance in the stone and earth bank moorland sheep had climbed in over the wall and it looked like the rank grass was going to support a ewe and two lambs whilst they grew fat.

'I would have cleared the plot sooner if you had helped,' I said defensively.

Our plot of land, Minions.

'Dylan has so far to go to school too. He can never join in after-school activities or have friends back and Max will be joining him there soon,' Bryn continued dredging up a favourite theme. 'Anyway, what will they do round here when they have left school? They'll never get jobs; unemployment is so high,' he finished, negatively.

'Well, actually I think we left it too late for this life-style to be a success,' I reasoned. 'The children had already got used to urban life and all it had to offer, shops, clubs, loads of friends. If we'd done it five years ago we might have stood a chance.'

'I think we've been rather naïve about it actually,' Bryn said after a sip of tea. 'We thought things might be different here, in the country, but all the kids have still got their smart trainers and fancy bikes. By all accounts some of them have a better television in their bedroom than we have here,' he expostulated jerking his thumb at our ancient set in the corner.

He had a point about all of this, of course; I simply didn't want to face up to reality.

'Well, what's to be done about it?' I asked, groaning inwardly and dreading the answer.

'I think I'll take a trip up to Evesham and Cheltenham; see if there's anything there again; go to the union office in Gloucester and suss things out.' He obviously didn't feel embarrassed to return to Evesham a third time, with his tail between his legs.

Five days later he was back, slightly refreshed from having seen lots of old friends but with no good news about work.

'We've got to get away from here; shall we put the house up for sale and see what the interest is? If we have an offer we can decide what to do next.' He was determined now that he'd felt the pull of pay in his pocket and been reminded of what we had given up.

Our house was put on the market and we sat with a map of England on our laps trying to decide where to go. Finally, after much deliberation we settled on Bristol – it was almost half way between our mothers' homes and our family connections and best of all we knew it already; at least, we knew the city centre and Bryn felt he would be able to find a job. It was a lively vibrant city and I guessed I would have to count my brief experience of country living as an experiment that went wrong.

We planned a house hunting expedition and Bryn checked the car over the week before we went. We had an ancient Vauxhall Viva now but it was already suffering from the miles we had put on the clock.

Our previous car had never quite recovered from a collision with a herd of runaway bullocks that we had encountered one foggy night when we were collecting Dylan from a Motorhead concert at the Cornwall Coliseum, a couple of days after his thirteenth birthday. The free-roaming cattle had decided to gallop off the moor down a bottle-neck between two walls and suddenly the leader loomed up just in front of the radiator. We had pushed our damaged car off the road into the bracken and walked home to phone the police as at the least one bullock was seriously injured. The next day a tractor towed the car home and Bryn had spent weeks patching it back together but although we did get it back on the road we never felt confident driving it and our old Avenger finally it made its last journey – to the scrap yard.

The Viva was deemed fit to make the journey to Bristol and we arranged for the boys to stay with relatives while we began the job of looking for a new home. The excitement of house-hunting had worn off now; we'd done it too often. This move would just be a practical solution to a financial problem and if we wanted to keep our new mortgage to the absolute minimum we knew any money we made on the sale would be absorbed in putting down a larger deposit.

We drove round the suburbs of Bristol moving closer to the city centre to achieve the price range we could afford. Easton, Lawrence Hill, St George, we visited them all, dipping into estate agents for reams of particulars. We wrote down a few addresses and started to construct a viewing list then moved on to St Werburghs, Brislington and Bedminster. We'd seen enough for day one and drove to our friends' house to form the short list. The following day was just as hectic as we kept one appointment after another until we had viewed all the houses we had lined up. We desperately needed a day off and drove up to Birmingham before collecting the boys from Redditch.

Back at home we'd had an offer on our house so we had to act quickly on the properties in Bristol and made offers on the three best. Months passed with the usual highs and lows of house sales and purchase but we were left with a feeling of deflation and depression. Our buyer had dropped out, we'd lost the Bristol houses and the whole process and the whole business had to start again.

Meanwhile, the UBO had insisted that Bryn should get a job, any job – they wouldn't pay our benefit any longer, and he started work at a local printers.

During the first week in August we made another trip to Bristol as our house was sold subject to contract. We would have one and a half days to find our new home so we were outside an agent in Bedminster when they opened. We couldn't see a house that was big enough at a price we could afford that was in a reasonable area. I felt low as we wandered the streets disconsolately dismissing house after house. We worked our way to Totterdown and called in for a snack to the wholefood shop in the Totterdown Centre and just as we crossed the road we saw another agent and scrutinised the window. Yes, there was one that might do: a bay-fronted terraced house in a road of identical houses but the price was cheap; only eighteen thousand pounds. It was empty the agent told us; we could have the key and go and have a look.

It had been unoccupied for some time and smelt musty; crystals had formed on some internal walls and the gas geyser over the bath had coughed up a black sooty deposit. However, it had potential; it would need hard work – which we could supply and it would certainly need money spending on it – which was a rarer commodity.

'What do you think?' Bryn asked doubtfully.

'The kitchen and bathroom need an update,' I confirmed glancing at the stained whitewood sink cabinet, 'but I expect we could do it bit by bit.'

'We need to find somewhere before lunchtime tomorrow,' Bryn added, stating the obvious. 'There's one other to view isn't there? Shall we look at that then come back here?'

'Let's walk down to the shops first and see what this neighbourhood is like. We know it's a walkable distance from the city and station,' I suggested.

Half an hour later we had satisfied ourselves that Knowle was a clean suburb with no evident vandalism. It had a library, swimming pool, cinema and park as well as a decent range of shops. The junior school wasn't far away and the Comprehensive was a mile down the A37. Later that afternoon, following our second viewing we decided it was the most likely house so far, and we'd better have it. We drove back to Cornwall relieved that our decision was all but made and on the following Monday we rang the agent with a firm offer. Nine weeks later we moved to Bristol.

Chapter 8

🍃 Maxse Road, Bristol 🍃

T his house was grotty; there was no getting away from it, and the building society's valuation report confirmed it. As usual we couldn't afford a survey but we didn't need one to see that the hot water geyser looked archaic, the kitchen was basic and dirty, many of the walls had evidence of damp and the whole place looked down-at-heel. Externally the house looked neglected; the window frames were in bad condition and the stone mullions and sills had started to crumble.

In its favour the house had three downstairs rooms in addition to the kitchen and three reasonable bedrooms too. We were great believers in the transforming effect of paint and paper and knew that our furniture and bits and pieces would give it style. In any case, after paying the bill for moving, plus solicitor's fees and all the other expenses we had put the rest of our surplus cash down as a deposit. We had to keep the mortgage to an absolute minimum; neither of us had a job. We had laid out eighty pounds on a smart VW Beetle which we hoped would be economical on petrol but this expense was a necessity; our old banger was in its death throes after another long journey up from Cornwall.

We had hoped to be in the house by the end of the school summer holidays so the children would stand a chance of making new friends at the start of a new session but already it was October and they would have to settle in after half term.

Bryn signed on at the UBO the following Monday and registered for work and for benefits. We confirmed that we had no money to buy school uniforms and made an appointment to see the Education Welfare Officer who provided vouchers to be exchanged for school clothes.

Two days after Dylan and Max started school Mum arrived to help me give the house a thorough clean before we started our unpacking in earnest. With her stamina fortified by a glass of sherry waiting on the mantelpiece of whichever room she was cleaning, Mum tackled all the dirtiest jobs and kept going for hours.

'Come on, take a break,' I would implore her. 'We can do that after elevenses.'

'I don't need coffee, I'll have a top-up,' came the reply as Mum stopped for a few seconds, wet cloth in one hand, a bottle of scouring cream in the other. 'There's no need to stop yet; when I've finished this I'll peel the potatoes and do the vegetables.'

'But Mum, you've been on the go since before the children went to school...'

'It won't get done if we keep having breaks,' she cut across me. 'You may as well make use of me while I'm here. Before I get the coach home on Sunday we'll go right through the house.'

In the evenings when we finally sat down, exhausted, Mum sometimes reminisced about the times she and Dad struggled in similar circumstances. They'd had very little money and for years no home to call their own; she told the stories graphically, emphasising the way the two of them had worked side by side to keep the family together and make our rambling house in Redditch into a home – the house that Dad had secured through tenacity, badgering the council daily to find somewhere so he could bring Mum and us children up to the Midlands to live. Bitterness was evident in these tales Mum recounted; fate had struck her some cruel blows, her life hadn't been easy but together they had got through the worst only to leave Mum widowed at fifty-six.

There was always a hint of a dark secret when Mum sat wistfully gazing out of the window as she re-lived her past. I knew by now that she had been married to a man who ill treated her but she kept this aspect of her past firmly locked in the closet – and of course, it was the part I wanted to know about for I wondered if it would hold the key to Mum's complex personality. I decided to begin jotting down these stories and before I went to bed I would scribble notes as reminders of the tales Mum told. Sometimes I would tape our conversations on my cassette recorder shoved behind the sofa, then later would transpose them into a notebook thinking that one day I may write a book.

Listening to these stories made me rethink my own marriage; things would be better from now on, I thought. Bryn had got what he wanted; we had moved to a city. He would soon find a job and I might look for something part-time and between us we would turn this house round to be a smart comfortable home.

Maybe I had been selfish, I acknowledged, but here I wouldn't have any distractions; I would live happily with a husband who loved me. After all, he was the same man I had married eighteen years ago; sensitive, artistic, well read, and a pacifist. Surely I was being silly to feel that my husband's love was too demanding, claustrophobic and intense. I was lucky to have someone who cared for me but the feeling that I was being controlled persisted; I felt like a puppet dancing to some-one else's tune.

During those early days in our new house, with time on my hands, I realised that I wouldn't be able to cope with the inconvenient and outdated kitchen. We bought a cheap stainless steel sink top and I drew up a design for a wooden unit to house it and provide shelves under the plank work-top. I didn't feel able to make and fit doors so I bought some fabric to match the curtains and gathered it up on wires stretched across the front. Fired up by the success of this simple project I made a pine work top over the washing machine with a wide shelf at the back for my crock storage jars. My woodwork lessons in Evesham had given me the confidence to have a go and these basic units lasted for many years.

Meanwhile we started to settle in. I joined the local branch of the Labour Party and was soon voted minute secretary. I walked down to Ruskin Hall in Brislington with George who became a good friend for the rest of my life. Bryn joined CND and we all started to go to the local Methodist Church nearby, on the Wells Road. In mid-December we visited Bryn's mother in Torquay and enjoyed seeing friends and family. Christmas loomed with all the expense that it would bring and we didn't look forward to it for we had no money to spend on gifts and festive food. There had been no jobs for Bryn to apply for and the time of plenty that we had anticipated was not about to begin. I saved up some of the family allowance and put by a little of the house-keeping money to insure that the children had presents and we managed a basic Christmas dinner with a small coal fire burning in the grate. Over New Year we went to Redditch for four days and all crammed into Mum's small flat while she treated us to all the good things she could afford and we went home wondering what 1984 would bring for us.

'We must decide how we're going to cope,' I began, once the children had gone back to school. 'It's obvious that the job situation isn't what it was.

It wasn't many years ago when you could swop jobs almost on a whim – and you did, didn't you?'

'Don't start! We are talking about *now* not what happened fifteen years ago. I *want* to find a job now and I can't; how do you think that makes me feel?' Bryn snapped back, somewhat rhetorically, throwing his magazine down and re-crossing his legs in annoyance.

'OK, what if I look for a job and you stay at home keeping things going on the domestic front?' I suggested, thinking that this might be a solution to our financial difficulties. 'A sort of role reversal thing. We tried it a while in Cornwall and you enjoyed baking and changing the beds and doing the laundry,' I continued, seeing some potential in this set-up.

'Well, it might work, but would I have to do the ironing and cleaning too? I'm not too sure about those,' he hesitated.

'It would depend if I found a full- or part-time job,' I mused, secretly smiling to myself, for I knew that Bryn felt I had the easy option, staying at home, doing the chores. It was convenient for him to forget that I had always worked at some paid job except for a very few weeks just after each child was born.

'Well, I don't expect you'll have any more joy than I've had but you could look I suppose. What sort of work would you go for?'

'I won't know until I see it. I'll tackle anything as long as it's interesting. We'll just have to wait and see!' I answered feeling as if I'd won my point.

'I didn't have that option!' was Bryn's final comment as he picked up the Jazz Journal again and I turned into the kitchen to put the kettle on for coffee.

I began immediately to search the situations vacant columns of the Evening Post and after a couple of weeks I found a vacancy that looked interesting: Materials Negotiator for The Children's Scrapstore it said. A warehouse full of recycled material to be reused for children's craftwork, it hinted. I rang the number for further information and learnt more about this project. The Bristol store was one of a chain across the country that collected waste material from factories and businesses and passed them on to play groups, youth clubs or craft projects for them to create things from. They invited me to go down to the warehouse housed in an old factory building in Bedminster. If I liked the look of it I could complete an application form.

I cut across Victoria Park and passed under a railway arch following my A to Z. After negotiating several roads I walked across an old church yard to the corner where a red brick building loomed. Several recycling projects were housed in the warehouse and as I walked under a huge arch I saw a sign for Scrapstore on the left. A man was standing on the top of a high stack of boxes balanced on scaffolding planks and Dexion racking. All around were tins of paint and sacks, crates of assorted bits and pieces and sheaves of paper. In another area a huge figure was being constructed out of what looked like cigarettes and people were pushing trolleys round, filling them with bounty. One of the workers called hello and I told her I'd come about the job; to see how they operated.

'We work as a collective, with every member of the team helping to make decisions which affect the running of Scrapstore. There are about eight of us and Simon is the project leader,' the woman called back.

'Yes, but what do you *do*?' I asked, still none the wiser; all I had to go on was the info I'd been given on the phone.

'I'll see if Simon or Geoff is free, they've been here longest,' she replied descending from the tall step ladders where she'd been tidying shelves.

Fifteen minutes later with a cup of tea balanced on the edge of a full desk I was beginning to get a feel for the organisation of this vibrant project. The job advertised was known colloquially as The Scrounger and the main role was to persuade companies to give us their useful waste. The ways of making contact would be left to the scrounger; the chief thing was the materials must be safe and non-toxic. Once the deal had been arranged the van driver would add the collection to the weekly list of collections and the materials would be brought back to Bedminster. About four or five people worked in the warehouse on a part-time basis and they stacked and labelled the stuff, worked on the check-out and gave advice about the suitability of various waste products. In addition there was a craft worker and play-leader, and a couple of admin staff. Quite a set-up, I thought.

I loved the idea of making waste things into play things and said I was interested in the job so Simon passed me an application form which I completed there and then. The scrounger's job was full-time, forty hours a week so I would need to get organised at home and have some answers ready for my interview in three day's time.

Later, in the cool of the huge building with four members of the team sitting informally in a semicircle I fielded the questions at my interview.

To sum up everything we'd discussed up a tall man with worn jeans asked,

'So you wouldn't mind handling things that had been chucked into a skip or piled in a dirty corner of a factory?'

'Oh, no' I confidently replied, remembering my days at auctions rootling through boxes and as a cleaner and gardener, dairy-maid and veterinary nurse. 'In fact I have an affinity with bins!'

A titter rippled round the group and the interview was over. I walked back through the park where bulbs were emerging through the grass under the trees and walked slowly up the Wells Road to home. I'd only been home for half an hour and the phone went. I was offered the job with a starting pay of £100 a week.

'But what will it mean to us all as a family?' Bryn questioned. 'You'll have to leave at seven-thirty to walk there for eight o'clock.'

'Well if you woke the boys up as I left the house then sorted out their breakfast and got them off to school you would be able to get on with the household jobs quite early,' I replied, feeling positive. 'You could develop the same routine as I've had for years except you wouldn't have a part-time job to go to.'

'Hmnn,' mused Bryn, 'I'm not sure if I'll be able to do all the things you did nor in the same way.'

'There's no mystique about housekeeping,' I responded patiently, 'it just needs some organising. Once you've broken it down into shopping and cooking, washing and ironing, and cleaning and tidying it will all fall into place. A hundred pounds a week is good money so it's worth giving it a go – anyway my contract is only for a year. Are you up for the challenge?'

'Oh yes, OK,' Bryn sighed. 'I've been looking for a job for six months and haven't come up with anything. Yes, go for it!'

On Monday 5th March I began my first full-time job since the children had been born. I loved the varied work, not knowing what each day was going to throw up but most of all I enjoyed working with the team; the camaraderie, the banter, the different personalities.

Over the next few weeks other new members of staff were taken on as previous contracts expired and as more funding became available from the Manpower Services Commission who paid our wages. Newcomers Clive and

Beni became close friends across the years and Una, Jude and Mike joined Simon, Geoff and Rob to form the new team.

The person I worked most closely with was Jim, the van-driver, and during the two or three days a week that we drove round Bristol collecting waste materials we developed an affinity, a way of working together symbiotically that required no detailed instructions or elaborate explanations – we were on the same wavelength.

Some days when there wasn't much on our collections list we would bunk off. Jim, true to anarchist ideology would deem it our due; after all we were working for a project that had been created to manipulate the unemployment figures so we were under no obligation to work solidly all the time. Some days we would take the scenic route back home and pull in to a lay-by and go for a walk or one memorable day we stopped at Priddy ponds on Mendip and Rob and Jim went skinny-dipping. On other days we would call at the Well Woman Clinic where Jim's friend worked and scrounge a cup of tea or call for a chat with the co-workers at the Wholefood Co-op. Usually when we had time to spare we would call at Jim's flat and he would make us a cuppa while I sat on a floor cushion listening to reggae or African music – sounds I'd never heard before.

As we worked together we discussed many fascinating topics and Jim put a new slant on several issues that were uppermost in my mind. One of them was religion; I had become disenchanted with formalised religion and my membership of the Methodist church – it simply didn't fit in with all the other new ideas I was taking on board. I borrowed two books which gave me another take on religion, amongst other things, and I pored over *The Paradise Papers* and Eva Fige's *Patriarchal Attitudes* taking in new concepts that became part of my ideology. I came to believe that religion had been used across the centuries to control people and in any case was a culture dominated by men.

I also read books that reinforced my new ideas about a woman's role in the home and *Kitchen Sink or Swim* by Deidre Sanders with Jane Reid which explored the theme of women and work, and also Ann Oakley's *Housewife* were both influential in my thinking.

Meanwhile, my love of planning hadn't gone to waste and I thought of various campaigns to draw attention to the work of Scrapstore and encourage businesses to offload their usable waste materials to us.

Sometimes we leafleted an industrial estate and asked them to ring us if they thought they were throwing away anything we could use; we suggested that our craftworker could look at its potential. Sometimes we rang round the companies in a small estate and this direct contact often gave us some good contacts. If there was a big factory which I guessed put loads of waste products in their skips I would make a personal phone call to the manager and arrange to meet up to suss out the usefulness of anything recyclable. Usually we just blitzed an area and snooped in the bins and skips.

Drawing paper, wallpaper, ends of rolls of cellophane and foil, foam, polystyrene and cardboard were all our stock in trade. To that we added empty film canisters, redundant tobacco tins, damaged tins of paint, tubing, racking and wood. We visited factories that made modelling clay, haberdashery, carpets and underwear to claim items that had been destined for the skip.

Dylan, 1984.

I soon consolidated my knowledge of Bristol and under Jim's tutelage learnt the connecting roads that linked the suburbs as well as the radial roads of the city. I drove the Transit van some days and learnt to judge the extra width of the vehicle and how to reverse into narrow spaces using the wing mirrors. I woke every morning with a sense of anticipation and looked forward to my day's work with excitement.

At home Bryn was coping with the domestic arrangements and managing to find time to do some baking as well as listening to music, sketching and reading in his leisure time. However, underlying this I sensed a discontentment, a vulnerability. I shrugged it off telling myself that he'd had ample opportunity to find a job; it was getting on for five years since he'd worked. Since the early seventies he had encouraged me to get involved in Women's Liberation and to play an equal part in our relationship and this was how it was working out practically. But as I got stronger, both physically and emotionally, Bryn was becoming less confident and more inadequate. I found my respect for him was dwindling and his weakness irritated me. Mum would come down to Bristol on the coach for a long weekend and couldn't wait to metaphorically stab Bryn in the back.

As May turned into June all talk at work was of the Glastonbury CND Festival at Worthy Farm just outside the town of Glastonbury, famous for its Tor and stories of the Holy Grail. Scrapstore was running a food marquee on site and was looking for volunteers to staff the stall for the three days of the festival plus a day each end to cater for people working on site erecting tents and fences. I'd heard of the festival of course but with my fairly conventional life together with lack of money I never in my wildest dreams imagined ever going to a pop concert let alone a festival. I put my name down for the whole five-day stint and decided I would face the consequences at home.

Bryn was not happy; he said I would be letting him down – and the children. He wanted to know what the sleeping arrangements would be and who else was going. Thursday 21st June was Max's birthday and I promised to be at home for the family event.

Tension built as the weekend of the festival drew closer and at one stage Bryn said he would come too and bring the children. The day before I was due to leave a phone call from his mother stalled that idea and he arranged instead to spend the weekend in Torquay. That evening we stayed up late with Bryn wanting to talk. He said during the day he'd made a few decisions and he wanted to try and change himself to fit in with me and the changes he felt I'd made in my life.

'Surely any changes you make should be for you, not for me,' I interrupted gently. 'If you aren't happy with your life then of course try to do something about it.'

'I can remember all your comments from when we last had this discussion two years ago,' Bryn said ruefully.

'Exactly, and I haven't altered my opinion,' I responded. 'I have made some radical changes to my life and the way I see things. I felt I just wasn't being true to myself – and you encouraged me most of the way!'

'I didn't know it was going to go like this; I feel left out and left behind.' The emotion mounted as we put our feelings on the line. 'I can see that in your work situation you can rely on others for emotional and spiritual support and I feel you don't need me,' he continued.

Max, 1984.

'Yes I suppose the first bit is true,' I conceded, 'but change won't happen to you unless you put something into it and be open and relaxed enough to take something out of a discussion.'

'I think it might happen if I ever have the opportunity to work on a scheme similar to yours and with a nice bunch of people that I can trust,' Bryn concluded with a wistful sigh.

The next day was Max's birthday and he went to school very excited about his presents and looking forward to his birthday tea. At work the van and hired vehicles were packed up with tents and provisions for the food stall and departed for Glastonbury, promising to return in the evening for the quota of helpers.

On several occasions we had practised erecting the huge poles and hauling the folded canvas up on the pulleys before stretching it to full size with the smaller posts round the edges. The old church green just along the road was big enough for this dry run and we had picked the sunniest afternoons in the preceding weeks. Now it would be for real. At seven o'clock the van pipped its horn outside the house and I slung my sleeping bag and rucksack in the back as I kissed goodbye to Bryn and the children and hopped up into the front seat.

Much later that evening eight of us sat around inside the Scrapstore food marquee drinking mugs of tea. Camping gas lamps illuminated the scene as the power wasn't on yet: the junction boxes weren't wired up. It was hard to believe I was finally there at last. The smells were wonderful: great baskets of fresh fruit each side of the tent and people had been cooking veggie-burgers and delicious greasy smells were wafting over from the stove. Music was pumping away on all sides together with the throb of the generators and the hum of the power cables. People were tapping away, putting up the last of the stalls and I could hear isolated pockets of chatter.

It was almost midnight and outside the mist was creeping up the valley and plumes of smoke from the camp fires were going straight up into the breezeless night. Huddles of people crouched round the fires smoking joints and hurricane lamps hung on tent poles casting a glow over the enchanting scene.

It was a cool evening and I hoped my three woollen army blankets heaped on top of me would be enough in the tent I was to share with Elaine. Our little encampment was in the Green Field about ten minutes walk away and we had put up bundles of coloured rip-stop fabric in the hedge to decorate our site. It would soon be time to make our way over to the tents but everyone was reluctant to make the move for bed. We put out the food in readiness for breakfast – huge boxes of cornflakes, bags of muesli, cartons of juice and plastic bowls in tall piles.

At last the electrics were switched on and a huge spotlight hung from the centre pole. In the stark light everything looked a bit of a muddle but a couple of the team had laid out the larder area and the preparation and cooking sections near the serving bar along the long edge of the marquee. I was immobilised with tiredness as I sat on the edge of a trestle table and dangled my legs. I was feeling a bit shivery and had a job to believe I would warm up in bed.

I finally made my way to the toilet block past a tent where loud reggae beats were pulsing away and so back to my own tent. The valley looked magical; like nothing I'd ever seen before. It was quite dark with a clear sky and very, very bright stars. Lamps were lit everywhere and still the wood smoke was drifting along. I sat crosslegged in the opening of my tent aware that people were swishing through the long grass close by as I wrote my diary by torchlight.

It was a relief to get up in the morning although it was only five o'clock. I had lain there since three feeling cold despite being fully dressed in bed. The canvas had been flapping noisily in the gusty breeze and I had been aware of cars revving and movement all over the huge site. As I flexed my stiff limbs and peeped out through the flap I was surprised at the number of people coming into the site even at this early hour. I was on duty from eight o'clock and I willed myself to get another couple of hours sleep.

Friday was a long day with a six-hour shift in the morning and another six hours in the evening. Breakfast preparations went smoothly and once serving was over I helped make filled rolls and put cakes onto plates. During the last hour of my shift we started doing the vegetables for the evening meal and then I was free to relax. I listened to Billy Bragg then Hank Wangford. Joan Baez was next but I needed a rest before making my way to the food marquee at four. Once I had geared myself up for work I was going strong on adrenalin. A co-worker said I looked sparky and healthy – was I 'on' anything? she wanted to know. If truth be told I was fed up with hearing people talking about dope, let alone use it. The atmosphere was high with the smell of joints and one of the women said she thinks that it's the only way ninety percent of people there keep going – dashing out for five minutes every hour to roll one up. The skies turned iron grey and rain set in for the evening and the canvas flapped damply but spirits were high with a lot of customers coming into the marquee to shelter while they bought their evening meal. Black Uhuru were playing when my shift ended and I crashed out on a block of foam to listen to them before catching the last bit of Ian Dury's set.

The night ended with Doctor John playing his wonderful blend of belting R&B and rolling Louisiana-style piano. Although I was tired I had to stand up and dance. The beat of the blues music was compelling and a swirling glitter-ball and a laser show created a beautiful pattered effect across the huge area. The vortex of coloured blobs seemed to disappear into infinity as it mingled with rising smoke. I had a can of lager with my companion, Paddy, and admitted that I hadn't drunk alcohol for about three years. Eventually I meandered back to the Green Field and my tent to grab four hours fitful sleep before my early shift of cooking bangers, bacon and beans.

Sunday passed in a combination of work and leisure watching Nikki B, Restriction, the Lozenges and Fela Kuti and I knew the weekend would soon be over. On Monday the camp-site began to break up and we concentrated on using up the last of the food, making up salad-rolls for the departing hordes. We closed the food marquee at eleven and had a couple of hectic hours dismantling everything and stowing what we could in the first van load. Once it was unloaded back at the warehouse I drove back to Glastonbury for more kit, not finishing work until six in the evening when finally I slammed the doors on the empty Transit and hung the keys on the nail.

Bryn was out painting when I got back to Maxse Road but once he turned up he told me how much he'd missed me and that he hadn't enjoyed being at his mother's. He had left the children with her and gone down to Cornwall seeking out old friends. He said he felt thoroughly depressed when he discovered how many of our friends were splitting up.

'I can see our relationship going the same way,' he said emotionally. 'I think we could save it if we talk things through with someone at this stage.'

I remained non-committal and was longing to go to bed.

'Do you still care about me? Shall we give it a go?' Bryn pleaded.

I should have qualified my answer but it would have taken another two hours.

'Yes, I care,' I replied, feeling so sorry that I might be at the bottom of his depression but at this stage I couldn't give him any answers.

'I've got the number of a marriage counsellor so if you agree I'll make an appointment,' he continued.

Eager to close the conversation and go to bed I said he could and went to sleep reliving my Glastonbury experiences.

The next day work took over: I was cleaning out the portable ovens, scrubbing pots and pans and sorting out the reserve stock of the Scrapstore; tossing barrels, sacks and tents across to Jim. I admired and liked Jim and felt closer to him than almost all the other staff so I was delighted when he paid me the compliment of saying I was one of the most able-bodied staff on the project, always there if there was something to be done, never moaning about an injured back when something needed lifting. I glowed with pride at the praise like a silly schoolgirl.

Bryn met me from work and told me he'd been for his first session of counselling. I didn't feel as though I needed any counselling; for me there was nothing wrong. I felt alive and confident. That evening at a Labour Party meeting I was told by a woman I hadn't seen for three months that I looked fit and well and she wasn't sure if I was the same woman she had once met.

My marriage was under severe strain – that was for sure. I confided in my close woman friend Beni. She was younger than me with a lively zany personality and her unconventional attitude and worldly wisdom gave her an edge that I admired. She was a good listener and would sometimes interject with an empathetic comment. I could trust her with my most personal thoughts and felt relieved that I could share the pressure I was under.

Working at the Children's Scrapstore had been something of a watershed for me and with the support of so many colleagues and friends I felt empowered to rethink my life and my relationship, examining it in minutest detail, laying it all on the line. The house moves, the jobs I had done out of necessity, Bryn's mood swings and perhaps most of all the feeling that I wasn't being true to myself. My emotions were running at top speed; fear of the future, regret, hope, happiness and most of all guilt. Was I just being a completely selfish woman? Shouldn't I just count my blessings? Where was this dissatisfaction going to lead? Increasingly I was beginning to feel that I needed to step back from the situation in order to sort out my feelings.

As the summer glided past I felt increasingly discontent. My two closest, oldest friends had both gone exploring the world. One was cycling round the globe in one direction and the other was travelling round the opposite way. Here was I stuck in Bristol, keeping the family afloat with my earnings and largely unable to make my own decisions. The chance of a holiday seemed a million miles away – unless I made it happen.

I couldn't go far nor be away for long; two or three nights at the most. A long walk somewhere with my tent seemed an exciting possibility and I could get out of the Bristol suburbs on a bus. The bus to Wells went along the main road a hundred yards from the house so I unfolded my Ordnance Survey map to scan the area. I would make mystical Glastonbury my destination and choose a route of byways and footpaths to reach the town erecting my tent on the way.

I put the outline of my idea to Bryn and I think he was glad to have some time on his own as the atmosphere at home was stressful – a couple of counselling sessions hadn't sorted out our problems. On the twelfth of August I clambered onto the bus ready for the first part of my journey to Chewton Mendip. Half an hour later I stood on the pavement in the village adjusting my rucksack. I walked uphill for an hour passing ferns on shady banks and drifts of late willow herb under tangles of fragrant wild woodbine. Already berries were turning red and hazelnuts were ripening in the scorching summer heat. I needed a rest; my pack was pulling on my neck and chest and with relief I eased the straps from my shoulders and sank to the grass to swig from my bottle of water and sit in the shade for an hour. Mid-afternoon I struck out across Mendip and climbed to the top of the highest of the Nine Barrows with the ground dropping away on three sides. The burial mounds were quite close together and arranged in a chain. A footpath across the fields took me to a similar chain half a mile away where rabbit scrapes covered the ground between poppies and cornflowers. Grass hoppers were chirping in the grass and thistle seeds were drifting along in the cooling breeze.

I walked across North Hill and descended to where I wanted to pitch my tent. I cut across peaty tufts of dried out bog and disturbed two fledgling skylarks who took to their insubstantial wings. As I neared the pond the air was redolent with the tang of wild thyme and the sweetness of gorse, and harebells trembled along with the sedges and bog-grasses. I wasn't the only one who'd wanted to escape to the country – masses of cars had pulled off the road and an ice-cream van was doing a brisk trade. I wanted to be near the more secluded pond but with hordes of people shouting and playing as they spread out their picnics I knew I would have to wait until they drove home to experience the silence and sanctuary I wanted.

I moved over the springy grass to explore the mine workings on the side of the hill where the circular remains of a tumble-down chimney stack and buildings that would have housed winding gear and pumping engines. Shiny, black, irregular clumps of solidified slag testified to a smelting process and I could almost hear the miners' voices calling to their mates at the end of a shift.

Only two or three people remained now, bathing in the pool edged with purple sedges and the magic did not descend on the area until seven o'clock when the last of the cars had driven off and the mud began to settle on the bottom of the pond. Huge black and gold dragonflies skimmed the surface of the water and fish rose to nibble at flies as half a dozen swallows swooped down, time after time, to take in beaks of water. A big fish suddenly rose out of the water, turned a somersault and flipped back in and I felt at peace. The sun had nearly reached the tops of the trees and was illuminating the last evidence of civilisation: cigarette ends, crusts of bread and toilet tissue strewn around spoiling this lovely place.

I erected my small ridge tent and crawled inside to relax only to hear someone's feet swishing through the reeds by the water's edge as I dozed off. Nearby voices woke me and I peeped through the flap to see two fisherman standing in the shallows casting their lines in the still water. They left at nine-thirty and at last I had this piece of countryside to myself and my thoughts as I snuggled into my sleeping bag.

Chattering starlings woke me at dawn as they greeted the day from the reeds where they had roosted overnight, then suddenly, whoosh, and the flock took off and the only noise was the gentle plop of fish and the soft calling of pigeons. By the time I woke properly the sky was dull and cloudy and I decided to get packed up. The tent was stowed just in time before the rain came down and I left Priddy in a gentle drizzle.

Following my map I took green lanes and footpaths across fields to the edge of the Mendip escarpment and looked down over Wookey and the lowlands as mist filled the valley. The hump of Glastonbury Tor beckoned me from the distant horizon and I walked steeply downhill past Wookey Hole and across country. Sun had started to filter through the clouds and as the heat built up I crashed out in a thistly field only to have a rude awakening when a tractor and muck-spreader turned into the gate.

I pressed on relentlessly until finally I reached Glastonbury, giving up my idea of camping in a field for another night. Wringing out my flannel under the cold tap in the loos I freshened up and had the first wash for two days. The Glastonbury Assembly Rooms were hosting a Festival and had called at The Scrapstore to sort out gold card, silver paper and rip-stop to decorate the premises. I made my way there and had a welcome rest and cup of tea in the shade before exploring the town with its wholefood shops, gothic giftshops and esoteric bookshops. Back in the café a couple of guitarists and a harmonica player were improvising a blues number and I sat down for a think. A quick scout round behind the church and around the abbey had not revealed anywhere to pitch my tent that night and I asked advice from a man I recognised from his visit to our recycling project. My relief was enormous when he said I could sleep at his house just round the corner and he took me round there and slung three cushions on the floor as a base for my sleeping bag. I managed to stay awake for the evening's cabaret performance but back at the house I slept for nine hours until his partner brought me a cup of tea.

The next day was the last day of my mini-break and I decided to ascend the Tor despite the misty weather. As I sat half way up the mound I could see for less than a mile. So far I had felt no mystery or magic – it was just hard work climbing the steep slope. The mist slowly cleared and the horizon came into view and I could take in the patchwork of small fields divided up by hedges. I picked out lots of mature trees dominated by ash and sycamore. The flat plain stretching out towards the Mendip Hills looked surprisingly lush considering the drought and herds of Friesian cattle grazed the succulent grass. Noises filtered up the hill from the lowlands; geese cackling, children's voices and someone hammering a stake. Swallows swooped round the Tor, skimming the grass for flies then darting upwards on air currents and I continued the ascent to the ruins of St Michael's church perched on top of this famous mound.

Later that day Rob would collect me in the van as he delivered some materials in the area and I knew my break would soon be over. OK, I hadn't cycled round the world, nor hitch-hiked across continents but I had been self-sufficient for four days, had made my own plans and followed them through.

I felt strong and contented and was not looking forward to returning to Bristol to sort out my marriage.

I had been working at Scrapstore for six months now and had got to know people working in the other projects that shared the building. There was a variety of personalities; bohemian, artistic, rough and ready, intellectual and articulate and I enjoyed the vibrant mix of backgrounds. We socialised at lunch break and sometimes went down to the pub for a beer. Sometimes I went shopping with Beni and with her encouragement I threw out many of my threadbare boring clothes and bought new black jeans, a sloppy-joe jumper and a denim jacket.

In late summer the music scene in Bristol seemed to take off and gigs were advertised in *Venue* magazine. One band I particularly wanted to see was playing at Bower Ashton on the campus of the Art College and I thought I'd drive across town to listen to them. The listing said the performance would begin at eight-thirty but I hated to be late so I thought I would aim for eight-fifteen – particularly as I wasn't sure where it was. Feeling nervous under my veneer of make-up and new trendy clothes I drove through Ashton Gate, up the hill to the college campus and into the car park. The tarmac was barren; the carefully marked out parking bays were empty; just a couple of vans over by the flat building. I suspected I'd come to the wrong place, but what to do next? I sat and studied the printed lists of venues; surely this was Bower Ashton? It was almost a quarter to nine and still the site was quiet. A man paused and eyed me from the corner of the car park as he unlocked the back of the van and I felt silly and conspicuous. Five minutes later and I had decided to investigate; I may be missing the band at a completely different venue. I pushed open the swing doors of the hall and glanced round. On the stage four men were unravelling yards of cable and positioning microphones and speakers. At the back of the room knobs and lights glowed from a huge black desk and I suddenly realised that they were setting up equipment for the band. Blushing slightly I stepped back into the foyer and feeling like the new kid on the block I pondered my naïve mistake. I scuttled back to my car and repositioned it in a distant space and waited for other people to arrive. By nine-fortyfive I could slip in unnoticed and I handed over my money and stood at the back trying to feel casual and wondered what on earth to order from the bar – I wasn't used to buying drinks. It was a relief when the support band started to play and I could weave my way into the crowd to enjoy the music without feeling that everyone knew this was the first time I had ever been out on my own to listen to a band.

I was able to buy a few new items for the house too, although most of my pay was needed for the mortgage and the children. The next month passed calmly and our nineteenth wedding anniversary approached. Bryn made me a delightful card; a combination of collage and pen and ink work, and two well chosen but inexpensive gifts. I felt a fraud; I didn't deserve them when my feelings were so negative and felt it put pressure on me to return the affection they represented.

In the evening Bryn reiterated his love for me but I felt unable to verbally return it; I didn't know what I wanted let alone what to do next. We went to bed with a row festering and lay with our backs turned towards each other. I tossed and turned for hours with one thought continually resurfacing: Bryn no longer played a significant part in my life. I had outgrown him and felt self-reliant financially, practically and emotionally. He hadn't been able to keep up and I didn't need him any more. How on earth would I work through this? How could I be so callous and unfeeling to tell the person I had once loved and respected that he was no longer required? Was I sure about my feelings? – after all he had never ill-treated me, nor cheated on me. He loved me still and wanted to save our marriage but I felt I couldn't put any more into the equation; I would somehow go it alone.

The next morning I felt exhausted; my nerves were frazzled and I felt sick with anxiety in the pit of my stomach. I would bide my time for the right way to approach this delicate subject. Meanwhile I would talk things through with my closest and most trusted friends and see if I was being a fool.

A few weeks passed and I felt I had to give it a go. I wouldn't burn my bridges but I would step back and take an objective look at my life and my marriage although I was almost certain that essentially my marriage was over. Where would I go? How would I find a place to live? Could I afford it? What would I tell the children? Through my contacts at work I had heard of housing associations but I would need to sign up for a permanent tenancy so that was no good. Perhaps I could rent a room in a shared house, or a bed-sit? I didn't have a deposit to put down on a room, the money I earned each week was only enough for our immediate needs and neither of us had any savings – we'd always led a rather hand-to-mouth existence. The thought of sharing with someone was not something I looked forward to; I'd had my own home for nineteen years and already I'd dismissed the idea of communal living when the subject was discussed years ago.

Jim told me about a housing association called Self Help which provided short-term emergency accommodation for people who were desperate but I would need to complete an application form and go and state my case at a weekly meeting where the available properties would be allocated on the basis of need. The houses were often ones that had been bought up by a regular Housing Association but until funding was available to do them up and offer them on a regular tenancy – sometimes in the next financial year – they were sub-let to Self Help. I walked down to their offices one day and asked for a form. The receptionist told me not to get my hopes up; there weren't many properties in stock and a lot of people were after them. She also said not to expect too much from the houses themselves, after all most of them needed major works.

For four weeks I took time out of work and went to the depressing office with its tatty chairs and grim décor to beg for a house or flat. I had to explain my situation in detail and try to persuade the allocation officers that I was desperate. I also insisted on somewhere with two bedrooms as I felt I had to offer the boys somewhere to sleep if they wanted to come and visit me – it was essential to maintain a good relationship with my children although I guessed it would be under severe strain. Eventually I was rewarded by my plea reaching the top of the list and I was offered a shared house at Totterdown and for the time being at least, I would be the only tenant.

I braced myself to tell Bryn what I had done and how I saw it as a positive move that would help me put everything in perspective. He remained unconvinced and I think he realised that it would turn into a permanent separation. Emotionally he asked me to reconsider my actions and told me he would change but I remained focused on my decision and steeled myself to see it through without being swayed.

I had the keys in my handbag and had already been to look at the house. The housing association expected me to take up the tenancy straight away; after all I had said my situation was desperate. Later that evening I began to pack my clothes into the big expanding suitcase and shoved my soap-bag into a corner. I put some bed linen and a couple of towels into a shopping bag and said I would drive round the next day in the Scrapstore van to collect them. I decided to take my big pine chest of drawers that Dad had paid thirty shillings for years ago and I would heave the spare mattress downstairs tomorrow. The air was tense and we both felt choked with emotion. My heart was pounding and I was shaking slightly at the thought of this momentous life-altering decision.

The next day I drove the van up to the door of our home and was relived to find that Bryn had taken himself off somewhere while I packed my things into the back of the vehicle. I had told the boys as much as I thought they need know and promised to come to tea in a couple of day's time.

Chapter 9

🌿 Hill Street, Bristol 🌿
– and back to Maxse Road

Here I was in a squalid, damp and dirty house with a choice of taking upstairs or down. I chose upstairs and before I could put my mattress on the floor I had to borrow a broom and a mop and bucket from work and give the place a good clean out. The bathroom was pretty disgusting too and I thought I may as well invest in some cleaning materials from the corner shop. I strung up the curtains that I'd brought from home and made my bed up with clean fresh sheets. There wasn't much else to do except unpack my clothes and put them in the drawers and hang a few coat-hangers on the back of the door. I rigged up my reading lamp that I had remembered at the last minute and switched on the comforting glow. There was a fireplace in my bed-sitting room and tomorrow I would bring some scrap wood from work; a good fire would help to dispel the damp smell and take the chill off the unused room and at the weekend I would paint the walls with some of the scrounged paint. I drove back to work feeling weird and a bit panicky but my friends all grouped round to congratulate me on my courage.

My tenancy was for three months and covered the worst of the winter months. I got used to wearing layers of thick clothing and sitting in bed with my hands round a mug of scalding tea, my hot-water bottle at my feet. It wasn't hard to come by furniture with a job that involved looking in skips and a furniture recycling project in the same building so I added an easy chair, a storage cupboard and a wooden garden bench to my interior. I painted the bench with a huge red sunburst to match some cheap material that I used to make up foam-stuffed cushions and this did as my sofa. I added a battered fridge to the cooker that was in the kitchen and together with a rickety table and a couple of pine chairs I had the makings of a usable kitchen. It was a challenge to exist without the trappings of the consumer society and I had to exercise all my artistic skills to make this grotty house into a temporary home.

Back at work next week my friend Clive told me there was someone who wanted to buy me a cup of tea at break time. Who on earth could it be I wondered? Clive said it was someone who shared the same interests – he'd told them I was artistic and appreciated jazz and poetry and read a lot. I wasn't sure what to do; I felt I wasn't ready for this: but what harm could a cup of tea do? After a couple of prompts I gave in and shared my tea break with a man from another recycling project. Yes, we did seem to have a lot in common and he talked in a knowledgeable and articulate way. He wanted us to meet up again but I felt wary and didn't enjoy the feeling of being pursued – yet I felt flattered too. I kept a low profile for a week or two then one day just as I was leaving work I saw him sheltering in the entrance from the rain. With a rueful look on his face he told me he'd missed his bus and would have to wait some time for another. Feeling sorry for him I suggested that he came home and had a cup of tea with me and caught a later bus. That was the start of it; OK I shouldn't have done it; I know now that I shouldn't have given him any encouragement if I wasn't sure – but I did. Hours later with it still pelting down with rain and his last bus missed he asked me if he could stay the night.

'Don't worry Angie, I shan't seduce you,' he said with a grin and his special innocent look.

'You won't get a chance,' I replied, thinking quickly of putting him on the mattress in the other room. I had never been in a situation like this and was unprepared; a wave of vulnerability washed over me. I had been faithful to my husband, the only person to see me in bed and I felt self-conscious but I wondered if this was how the world at large lived. I was inexperienced and naïve but a faint excitement glimmered as I agreed to him staying over and I felt a woman of the world; in charge of my own destiny.

We saw each other at work over the next few days and I felt flattered that someone fancied me. He asked if I would like to go a walk on Sunday and have a cup of tea at his bedsit; I'd never seen anyone's bed-sitting room; in fact I'd only just found out about them so after our walk across the Downs the following weekend I stood behind him at the side door of the house where he lived while he pushed the key into the lock. The house smelt frowsty and unaired; a smell of cooking and bathrooms lingered in the thick air as he opened the door to his domain. There was a semblance of order in the room with mugs and cooking utensils hanging in the kitchenette and storage jars on a shelf unit. A plaster cast of a nose hung on the wall and other quirky artefacts were dotted round the room disguising the lack of space and underlying muddle.

We sat around cradling mugs of tea to ward off the cold in this damp and chilly room. As the evening drew on he slipped some coins in the meter and put the fan-heater on. We were absorbed in a conversation about art and music and literature and I was reminded of my early days with Bryn and the special feeling when you find someone on the same wave length.

'You'll have to run to catch the last bus,' he said glancing at the clock. 'Or you could stay the night here.'

'I'm not sharing a bed with you,' I replied, my eyes flicking over to the far side of the room where an untidily made double bed was pushed against the wall.

'No need! I've got an air bed up on top of the wardrobe,' he countered.

'OK, I suppose so,' I agreed somewhat reluctantly as I realised there would soon be no turning back. The fuggy comfort of the room and the pulse of the R&B music on the turntable finally persuaded me and I stood by while he climbed on a chair to reach up to the dusty collection of objects shoved in on top of the cupboard.

Over the next few weeks our friendship developed into a relationship and my life suddenly became more complicated. I was working full-time so I had to fit my domestic arrangements into the evenings; it was winter and bad weather increased the difficulties of shopping and drying washing. I had an on-going commitment to my children and visited them a couple of evenings a week when I would stay with them while Bryn went out. Sometimes the atmosphere was rather strained as they asked me when I was coming home. I tried to be honest with them without saying anything damning about their father but I often ended up stalling their questions by changing the subject.

On other evenings I visited my friends or went out to meetings or for a drink. Christmas was on the horizon and party invitations were coming in. I went on a pre-Christmas visit to Mum in Redditch and told her that I believed our marriage was on its last legs. A week later we all went to Torquay and it must have been evident that things were under strain; after all, by now we had been to our solicitor and registered a formal separation.

It was against this background that I had begun a new relationship and it wasn't always easy going. My new boyfriend had a complex personality. He undoubtedly had charisma and charm; that was what had attracted me but he described himself as neurotic and when the veneer of self-awareness chipped away he was prone to moods of gloom and self doubt.

With a background of Fats Domino or Creedence Clearwater playing on the cassette player I would sit for hours in his bedsit listening to him expound his theories on personality, psychology, inter-personal relationships and moral values. He had a convincing and persuasive style and I found myself modifying some of my long held beliefs only to revert to my original stance once I had thought things through on my own.

Angie, Minchinhampton Common, 1985.

We spent days out walking round parts of Bristol I didn't know; the Downs, the Avon Gorge, Henbury, Clifton and Redland. We would venture into the surrounding countryside or explore the green walkways that snaked through Bristol. Two or three evenings a week we visited clubs and pubs in Bristol to listen to bands playing jazz or rhythm and blues and my companion would come into his own with his knowledge of style, influences and musicians. He had an encyclopaedic memory for the titles of tunes and loved to compile cassettes of his favourite tracks.

Christmas came and went and I glossed over my emotions when I spent the three days with Bryn and the boys. In the middle of January with the end of my house lease just a few weeks away we had a meeting to discuss the future.

'I strongly feel I ought to come back to the children,' I insisted.

'But where does that leave me? This is my house too,' Bryn questioned pragmatically. 'If as you have hinted, our marriage can't be retrieved how can we live in the same house? I don't think I could face it.'

'The way I see it there could only be four variations. Firstly we could patch things up and carry on as before – and I see now that isn't going to happen. Secondly we could split up and sell the house and never see each other ever again – which I think is unviable when you add the children to the equation. Next, one or other of us could live in the house while the other person moves to a flat – well, neither of us can afford to do that. Lastly we try to make a go of it, living here but having our separate lives and somehow organising independent living arrangements. What do you think?' I paused for breath after this long speech that I had rehearsed for days.

'Well... it might work I suppose,' Bryn mused. 'There would be a lot to work out financially, with benefits and the care of the children.'

'Yes, but we could do it if we wanted to make it happen,' I reinforced as positively as I could.

'Right, we'll give it a go but I'll need some time to get my head round the idea,' Bryn concluded. 'Let's have a coffee now that's over. We can talk about the details another time.'

The first week in February the lease on my shared house was up. I wasn't sorry; another couple had moved into the rooms down stairs and we didn't share the same standards of kitchen and bathroom hygiene. During the day while I was at work they sometimes helped themselves to my stock of firewood and eventually began to burn pieces they had torn off the garden shed. I thought it may only be a matter of time before the floor boards were yanked up.

The problem was we hadn't finalised the arrangements at Maxse Road and I arranged a two week extension before I finally loaded up my belongings in the van and moved them back to our house in Knowle. Whilst Bryn went on a week's holiday I re-established my relationship with my sons but it was on a fragile level and I hoped things would improve soon. I found it harder now to cope with my new relationship. My partner didn't have any responsibilities and couldn't always understand the difficulties I had organising my life to go out two or three nights a week. There was a lot of fun to be had and I accompanied my pleasure-seeking boy friend round the clubs and pubs of Bristol listening to such local bands as The Soulsearchers, The Yakometties, The Amazing Hotshots and The Lozenges.

My contract at Scrapstore was due to end the last week of March and I wondered how I could support myself. Not for the first time in my life I trawled through the Situations Vacant columns searching for a job. After five weeks of signing on at the Unemployment Benefit Office I secured a temporary job with Bristol Parks Department as a summer gardener.

It was a great job and I thoroughly enjoyed working once again with a gang of men. There made no concessions for me and I took my place in the team, picking up litter, cutting grass and trowelling in the bedding plants in the parks and roundabouts that comprised our central patch. It was hot work out in the baking sun day after day and I sported a pair of leopard print shorts and a man's vest as my work kit which looked rather incongruous teamed with my issue of steel-toe-cap boots and leather gloves. The job continued until mid-October and during this time I managed to juggle work, home and a hectic social life with weekends away, walks, films, music gigs and holidays.

There were pivotal moments during the first year of my new relationship when I should have followed my head and finished it.

'Do you love me?' he would ask.

'Um… yes,' I replied with my brain scrambling. Surely I *must* love him or I wouldn't be there. I'd *got* to love him or all this would be wrong. I was a person who didn't do things casually. I'd always thought things out carefully, weighed up each side, spent hours agonising over major decisions but here I was ruled by my emotions. I needed fun and excitement after years of a life filled by convention and I was besotted with this man who could offer me a good time. It was great to be admired and shown off to his circle of friends and I revelled in my new interests of R&B music and dancing uninhibitedly to the strong beat.

In October it was one year since Bryn and I had led separate lives and there could be no turning back. In any case, well before this time my carefully planned opportunity to disclose my affair to Bryn had been pre-empted by my new partner spilling the beans and finally my husband realised our marriage

Angie on holiday near Brecon, 1985.

176

was at an end. Early next year he moved into rented accommodation nearby and I made the disastrous decision to invite my partner to move in with me.

Eventually after a total of four years our relationship fizzled out. I was glad when it happened as I had been unhappy for some time. The situation at home had become tense; unsurprisingly the children could not come to terms with it but that wasn't all. I had put too many demands on my boyfriend to conform to my standards – emotionally, practically and financially and he wanted out. Quite frankly it was a relief; I couldn't cope with the strain of a relationship that was wrong for me but I didn't know how to end it. As the pressure built up I found myself weeping spontaneously as I walked to work or sat at my desk. I asked his long-standing friends for advice and sought clues to unravelling his complicated character and those who knew him best gave me some insights into his personality.

I had worked my way through four more jobs as diverse as a waitress, a canteen manager, a regular car-booter and an administrative assistant for the council. I had weathered the final trauma of my divorce which became absolute in 1987 and re-established a civilised life style. What I didn't want was the emotional switchback that our relationship had become; I needed to get my life back on track.

When he finally packed up his bags and left I knew it was best for both of us and I began a new chapter in my life reinventing myself, camouflaging the scars as the wounds scabbed over and sewing the experience into the patchwork of life.